MARK COURTNEY, THE POST-CRESCENT (APPLETON, WIS.)

This book is affectionately dedicated to the memory of Arthur Rothstein — photographer, editor, teacher — who died at the age of 70 at his residence in New Rochelle, N.Y., in November, 1985.

the best of
Photojournalism/11

An annual based on the 43rd Pictures of the Year competition sponsored by the National Press Photographers Association and the University of Missouri School of Journalism, supported by a grant to the University from Canon U.S.A., Inc.

Contents

Spot news	6-125
Canon Photo Essay	32
Features, portraits, illustrations	126-187
Sports	188-231
Judge's perspective	232
The winners	234
Index to photographers	238

BELOW, DENNIS McDONALD, BURLINGTON COUNTY TIMES (WILLINGBORO, N.J.)

THOMAS KELSEY, LOS ANGELES TIMES

Above, photographers scurry to greet the President at Los Angeles during the Christmas holidays.

Left, photographers cover Rick Springfield at Live Aid concert.

Preceding page, 45 of America's most famous pop stars raise their voices (and billions of dollars) for the world's starving people. (See p. 42)

PRECEDING PAGE, MAGAZINE PHOTOGRAPHER OF THE YEAR, HARRY BENSON, LIFE

FRONT COVER, DAVID PARKER, YUBA-SUTTER APPEAL-DEMOCRAT (MARYSVILLE, CALIF.) SEE PAGE 81.

BACK COVER, DENIS N. LAW, FLAHERTY NEWSPAPERS (SEATTLE, WASH.) SEE PAGE 187.

Cal Olson, editor
Joanne Olson, assistant

Copyright © 1986
National Press Photographers Association, Box 1146
Durham, N.C. 27702

Library of Congress Catalog Number: 77-81586

ISBN: 0-89471-469-4
(Paperback)
ISBN: 0-89471-470-8
(Library binding)

ISSN: 0161-4762

Printed and bound in the United States of America by Jostens Printing and Publishing Division, Topeka, Kansas 66609.

All rights reserved under the Pan-American and International Copyright Conventions.

The photographs appearing in this book have been used with the permission of the holders of the rights thereto and may be subject to separate copyright. All rights reserved. This book may not be reproduced in whole or in part, in any form, for any purpose, without written permission from the publishers and respective copyright owners.

Distributed by Running Press Book Publishers, Philadelphia, Pennsylvania. Canadian representatives: General Publishing, 30 Lesmill Road, Don Mills, Ontario M3B 2T6.

This book may be ordered by mail from Running Press Book Publishers,
125 South 22nd St.,
Philadelphia, Pennsylvania 19103.
Please include $1.50 for postage and handling.
But try your bookstore first.

For information concerning the Pictures of the Year Competition,
contact Charles Cooper, NPPA Executive Secretary, Box 1146, Durham, N.C., 27702

Cover design by Running Press.

Volunteers work shoulder to shoulder, searching for survivors in quake debris.

DAVID WOO, DALLAS MORNING NEWS

1985: A year of action, reaction

News and the photojournalist: It's an action/reaction relationship, and in 1985 photojournalists reacted to a surfeit of action.

Major international news stories have always generated coverage by wire services, magazines, and television networks. But 1985 found a growing number of American newspapers sending photographers and reporters to all parts of the world — Africa, Europe, the Philippines, Central America — not only for background stories, but to cover breaking spot news.

Stories of tragedy dominated that coverage. A wave of terrorism swept the globe, and Americans living and traveling abroad were particularly vulnerable. One news agency reported 169 acts of terror against Americans during the year, all but six occurring outside the United States.

The Associated Press called 1985 "a horrific year" for air travel. Some 2,000 lives were lost in a series of crashes. One of the most poignant: the crash of a chartered airliner that killed 248 American GIs who were homeward bound for Christmas.

Natural disasters in Mexico (an earthquake) and Colombia (a volcano) took the lives of thousands, while the violence resulting from South Africa's racial policies continued to generate news coverage.

At home, the plight of American farmers, whose high-yielding harvests helped sink them even deeper into debt, played ironic counterpoint to the famine that still plagued Africa.

Still, the news was not all bad in 1985, as Time Magazine noted. "1985 had its redeeming features, large and small: The Live Aid concerts, with an audience of a billion plus, to help Africa's starving; the athletes overtaking records; the winning smiles on the faces of a young princess and a recuperating President."

* * *

Leading The Best of Photojournalism/11 is an event that received some of the heaviest coverage given any event of 1985: the aftermath of two earthquakes that devastated Mexico City in September. More than 20,000 people were killed. But many victims trapped in the 250 buildings that were destroyed by the quakes were rescued by volunteers who came from 20 countries.

Right, rescue workers carry an 8-day-old baby from the rubble of Benito Juarez Hospital, five days after the building was destroyed. The child lived.

RIGHT, J.B. FORBES, ST. LOUIS POST-DISPATCH

MICHAEL WILLIAMSON, SACRAMENTO (CALIF.)
PAUL KITAGAKI JR., SAN FRANCISCO EXAM

Above, Photographer Michael Williamson made this photograph as the second quake rocked Mexico City. The quake registered 7.5 on the Richter Scale.

Right, the body of one of the estimated 10,000 persons who died in the second earthquake. The body was found in the ruins of a six-story apartment building.

Mexican tragedy

Left, volunteers form a human chain to remove the bodies of earthquake victims from one collapsed structure.

Below, a 26-year-old woman is rescued by Swiss and French volunteers after being trapped for four days in the rubble of a 14-story apartment complex.

THIRD PLACE NEWSPAPER PHOTOGRAPHER OF THE YEAR, ERIC LUSE, SAN FRANCISCO CHRONICLE.
SCOTT R. SINES, SAN ANTONIO (TEXAS) EXPRESS-NEWS

Mexican tragedy

New clothing hangs from protruding reinforcing rods in a building in Mexico City's garment district.

J.B. FORBES, ST. LOUIS POST-DISPATCH

A priest makes the sign of the cross over ice-packed bodies of quake victims.

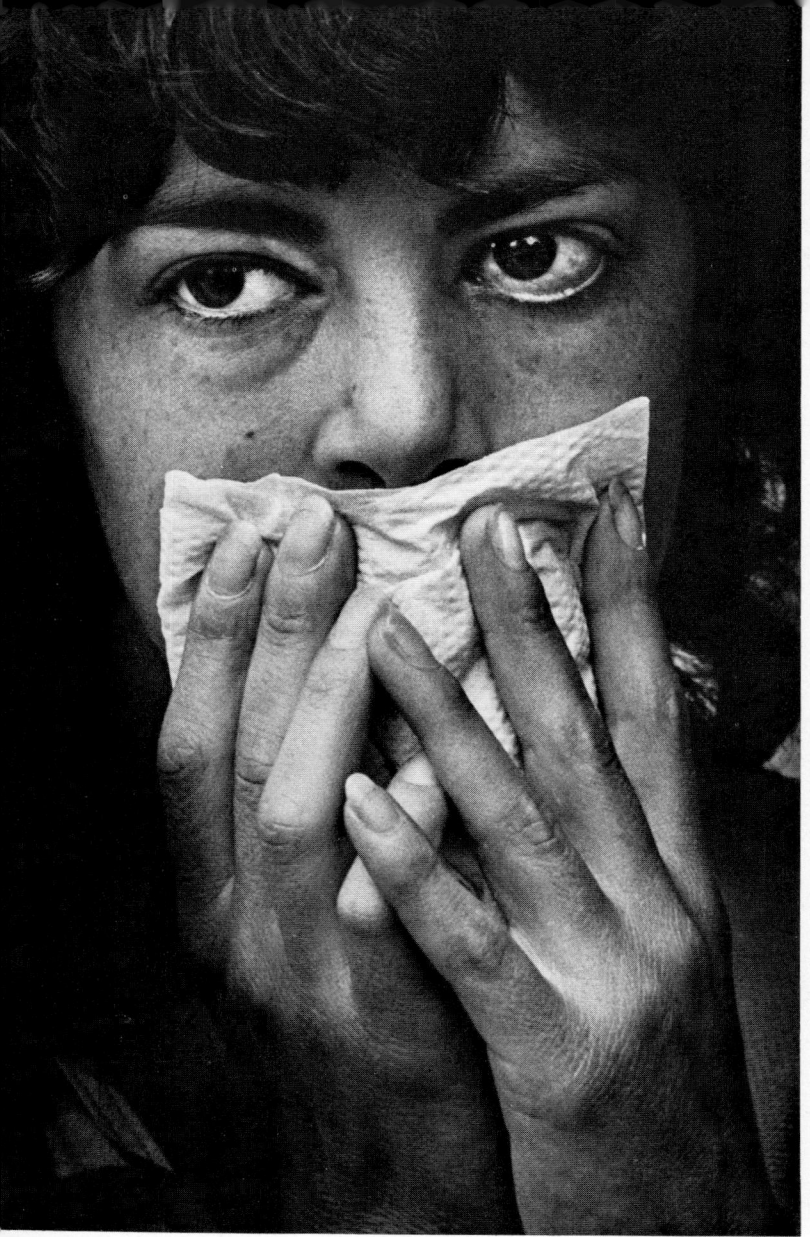

PAUL KITAGAKI, JR., SAN FRANCISCO EXAMINER

Above, a woman waiting for news of relatives reacts to the smell of death.

Below, survivors at the Benito Juarez Hospital in Mexico City, waiting for word of their loved ones, face the agony of covered stretchers.

THIRD PLACE NEWSPAPER PHOTOGRAPHER OF THE YEAR, ERIC LUSE, SAN FRANCISCO CHRONICLE

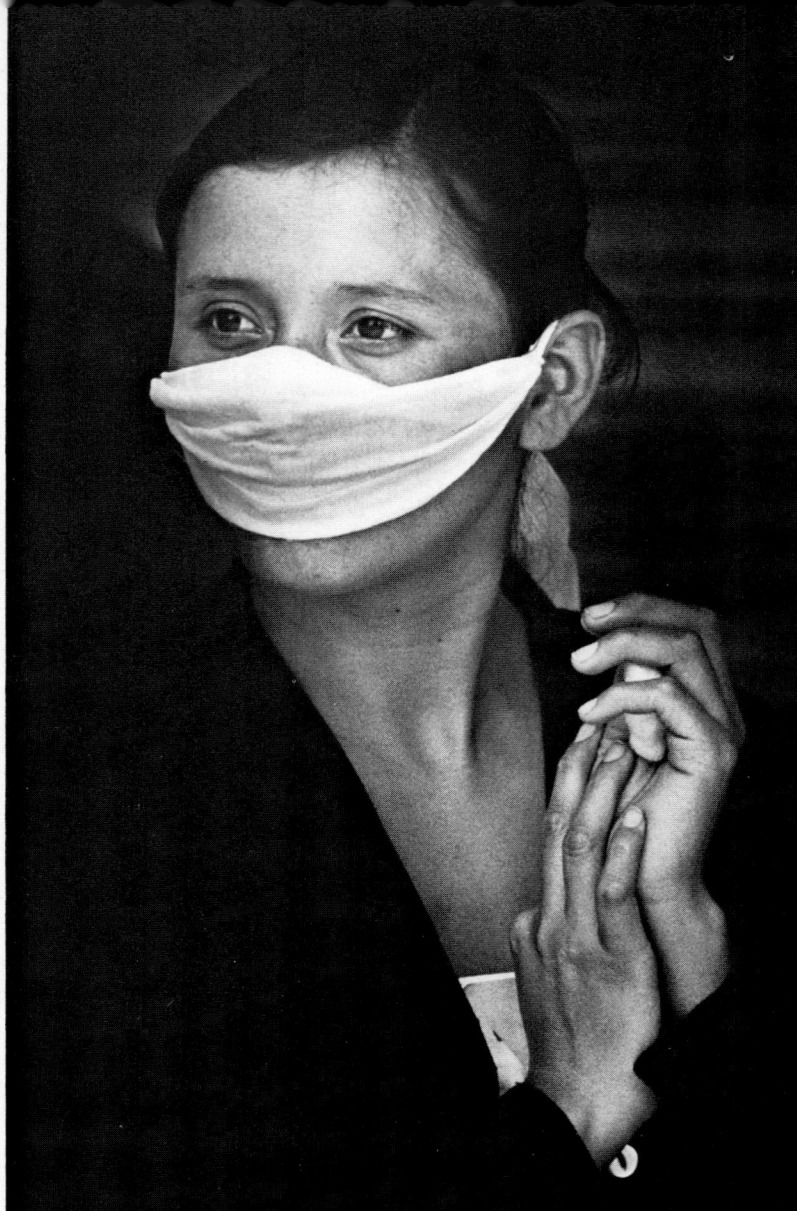

TED JACKSON, THE TIMES-PICAYUNE PUBLISHING CORP. (NEW ORLEANS, LA.)

Above, masked against the smell of decomposition, a woman waits outside a makeshift morgue in Mexico City.

Below, Lala Lopez was one of hundreds who went to St. Charles Catholic Church in San Francisco to pray for relatives in Mexico City.

DEANNE FITZMAURICE, SAN FRANCISCO EXAMINER

PAUL KITAGAKI, JR., SAN FRANCISCO EXAMINER

Above, relatives weep at the funeral of a quake victim.

Left, life continues for a 5-day-old girl found buried in the rubble with her mother. Both her parents died in the disaster. The baby was placed in an orphanage.

THIRD PLACE NEWSPAPER PHOTOGRAPHERS OF THE YEAR, ERIC LUSE, SAN FRANCISCO CHRONICLE

Mexican tragedy

Nightmare in Colombia

Colombia's time of agony came in mid-November, when the Nevado del Ruiz volcano sent a tidal wave of mud, ashes, and rocks smashing down from its 17,700-foot peak.

The town of Armero was one of four communities that were smothered in mud. More than 25,000 persons were killed, 8,000 of them children.

Help came quickly: U.S. military helicopters and transport planes rushed supplies into Colombia and helped move mud slide victims to hospitals.

Press coverage came quickly, too. Dozens of photographers and reporters were sent to Colombia. Their coverage brought offers of help from thousands of Americans.

Above, 36 hours after the Colombia volcano erupted, this man makes his way through the massive mud deposit near the town of Armero.
Below, 13-year-old Omayra Sanches died after 60 hours were spent in unsuccessful attempts to free her from the water-filled hole in which she was trapped..

Right, civil defense volunteers assist a young Colombian who survived the mud slide at Armero.

Far right, rescue workers attend the needs of a youngster found buried in the mud at Armero.

SECOND PLACE MAGAZINE NEWS/DOCUMENTARY, FRANK FOURNIER, CONTACT PRESS IMAGES

ANTHONY SUAU, BLACK STAR FOR NATIONAL GEOGRAPHIC

IRA STRICKSTEIN, THE HOUSTON POST

NURI VALLBONA, THE FORT WORTH (TEXAS) STAR-TELEGRAM

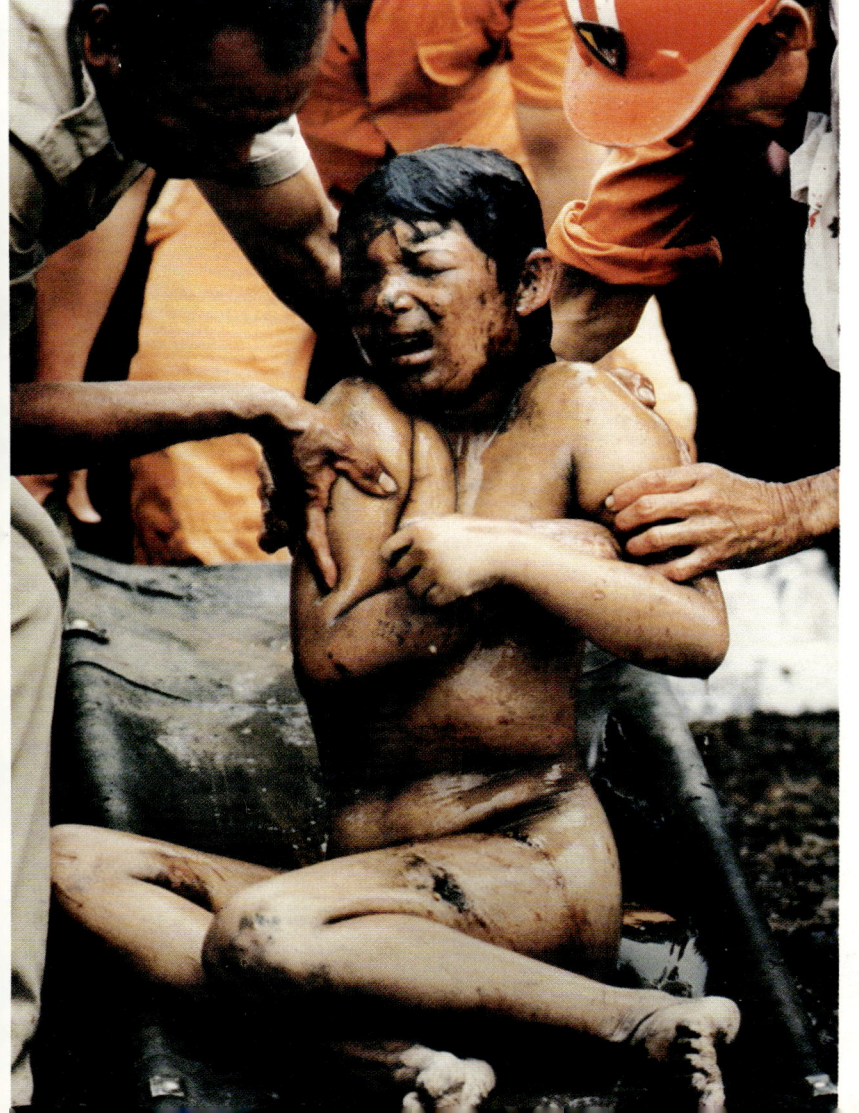

THOMAS E. LANDERS, THE BOSTON GLOBE

MICHEL duCILLE, THE MIAMI HERALD
EDUARDO GONZALEZ, ASSOCIATED PRESS

Upper left, a volunteer yells to alert medical personnel as he rushes a mud-covered child from a helicopter to a Colombian aid station.

Upper right, Colombian police chopper lifts a volcano victim from Armero's mud; this man had been trapped, covered in mud, for four days.

Right, dazed survivor sits atop his house in Armero, waiting for the next available Red Cross helicopter.

Colombian Crisis

CAROL GUZY, THE MIAMI HERALD

A dying woman lies amidst volcanic mud and Armero's rubble. Photographers Guzy and duCille (opposite page) shared a Pulitzer Prize for their Colombian coverage.

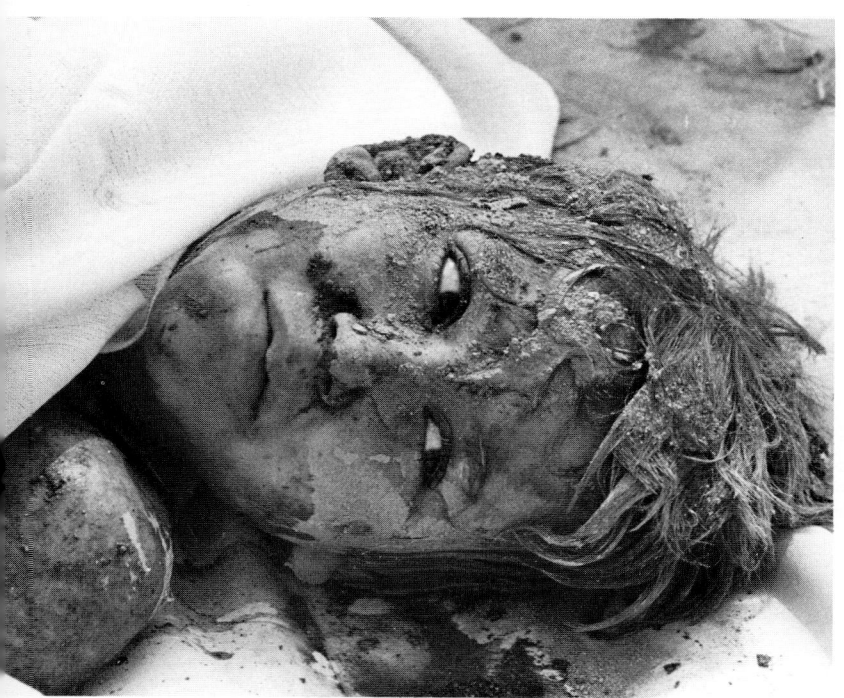

JIM WILSON, THE NEW YORK TIMES

RICHARD SCHMIDT, THE SACRAMENTO (CALIF.) BEE

Above, a young girl awaits help after being pulled from the mud.

Below, a badly bruised woman receives her first drink of water after being buried three days.

Above, 5-year-old Oscar Javier Vera is washed down to ease the pain of mud, gravel, and ash imbedded in his skin.

THOMAS W. SALYER, UNITED PRESS INTERNATIONAL

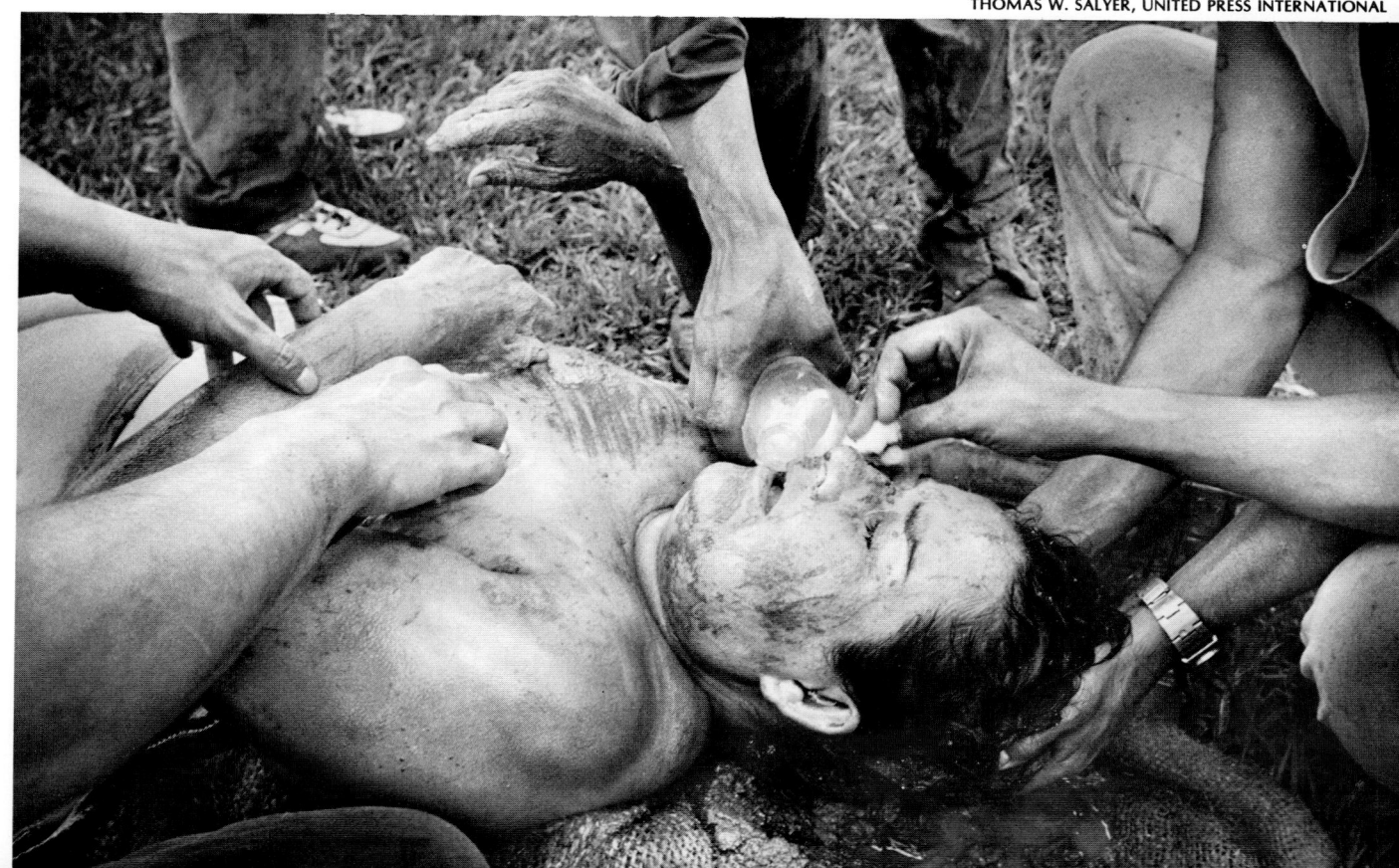

18

Above, after two days, rescue workers effected this man's release from the pervasive mud.

Below, an 18-month-old survivor of the tragedy cries in his hospital bed. Ten days after the mud slide, no one had claimed the child. He was given the designation "NN" (no name).

JIM WILSON, THE NEW YORK TIMES

Colombian survivors

JOANNA PINNEO, ASSOCIATED PRESS

JAY DICKMAN, DALLAS TIMES HERALD

In tiny Guayabal, the town square was used as a collection spot for the bodies of the dead. Here a grieving woman searches for the body of her husband.

Left, four days after the mud slide, the arm of a corpse sends a grim signal.

Below, so many deaths, so quickly; so little time, so little space. Bodies of victims were removed from their coffins and buried in a mass grave in Guayabal.

KATHY ANDERSON, THE TIMES-PICAYUNE PUBLISHING CORP. (NEW ORLEANS, LA.)

ED HILLE, THE PHILADELPHIA INQUIRER

Colombian requiescat

MOVE off

Pressed by West Philadelphians, police on May 13 confronted a militant, back-to-nature cult called MOVE.

When the confrontation was over, 11 MOVE members were dead (4 of them children), 53 houses were destroyed, and 250 people were homeless.

Right, MOVE members fortify a roof bunker. Below, cultist Mo Africa, who would die with 10 others in the siege and fire.

WILLIAM F. STEINMETZ, THE PHILADELPHIA INQUIRER
GERALD S. WILLIAMS, THE PHILADELPHIA INQUIRER

Police dropped a bomb onto roof of the MOVE house as the siege wore on. Here, police man a rooftop by light from the resultant fire, which burned out of control.

Below, two police officers rush into position as MOVE house burns.

GEORGE WIDMAN, ASSOCIATED PRESS (ORIGINAL IN COLOR)
VICKI VALERIO, THE PHILADELPHIA INQUIRER

MOVE's agony A West Philadelphia residential block goes up in flames.

BRUCE JOHNSON, PHILADELPHIA DAILY NEWS

Left, police work with crane to search for evidence in the burned-out neighborhood.

CHUCK ISAÁCS, THE PHILADELPHIA INQUIRER

GEORGE WIDMAN, ASSOCIATED PRESS

ove, the search for evidence continues at the scene the MOVE confrontation.

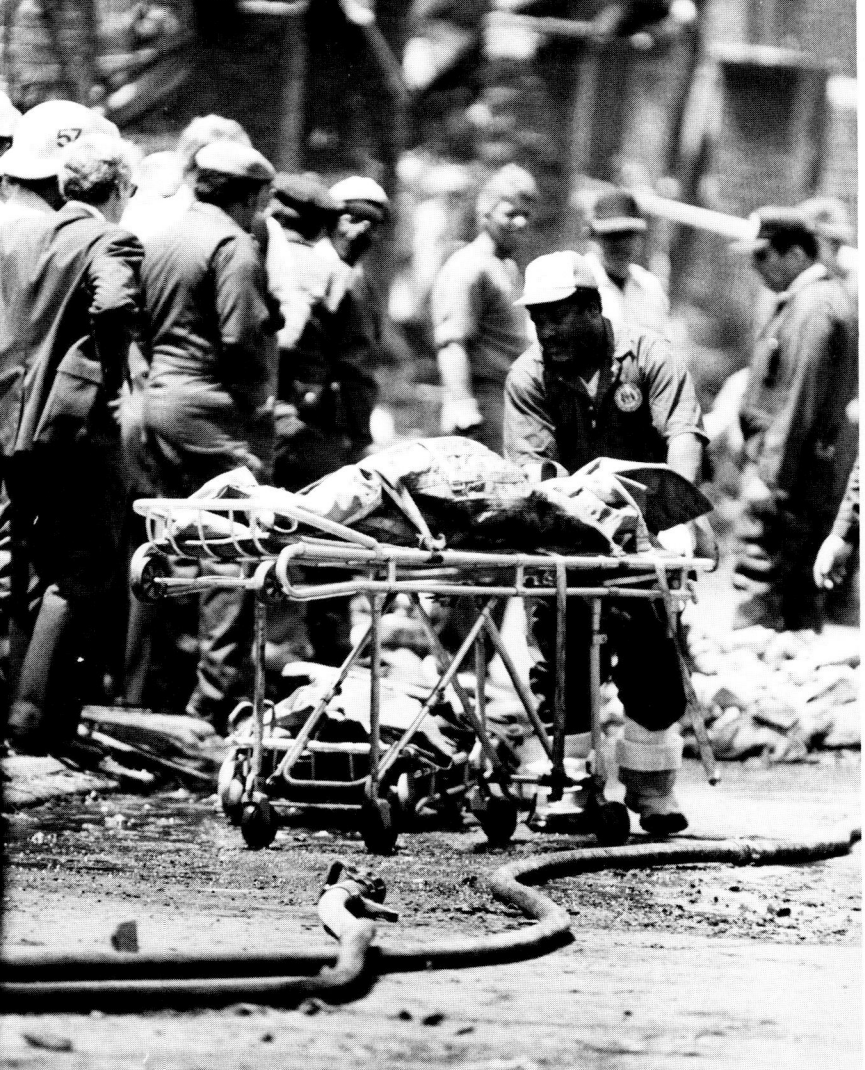

GEORGE WIDMAN, ASSOCIATED PRESS

Above, a worker pushes a stretcher bearing a body recovered from the MOVE house.

VICKI VALERIO, THE PHILADELPHIA INQUIRER

MOVE aftermath

Above, family whose home was destroyed visits the street one last time before houses are razed.

Below, this is how MOVE area looked June 10. Residents were promised rebuilt houses by Christmas.

AMY SANCETTA, ASSOCIATED PRESS

REBECCA BARGER, FREELANCE FOR THE POTTSTOWN (PA.) MERCURY (BOTH PHOTOS)

Above, MOVE sympathizers gather near the sheet-covered remains of John Africa and Frank Africa during graveside rites.

Left, this woman is one of the 250 West Philadelphians left homeless by the MOVE confrontations.

27

ORVILLE MYERS, JR., MONTEREY (CALIF.) PENINSULA HERALD

Rock Hudson's last public appearance came July 15 in Pebble Beach, Calif., to promote Doris Day's new television series. He died Oct. 2.

AIDS: Concern grows

The death of movie star Rock Hudson riveted attention on the AIDS epidemic, which through 1985 had claimed 14,000 victims, of whom half have died.

Reported Associated Press: The disease "frightened ordinary Americans, caused near panic in high-risk groups, and galvanized the medical community, which estimates the virus has infected half a million Americans."

As the incidence of AIDS grew, so did the controversy: Should children with AIDS be permitted to attend school? Should AIDS sufferers be quarantined? The national concern continues.

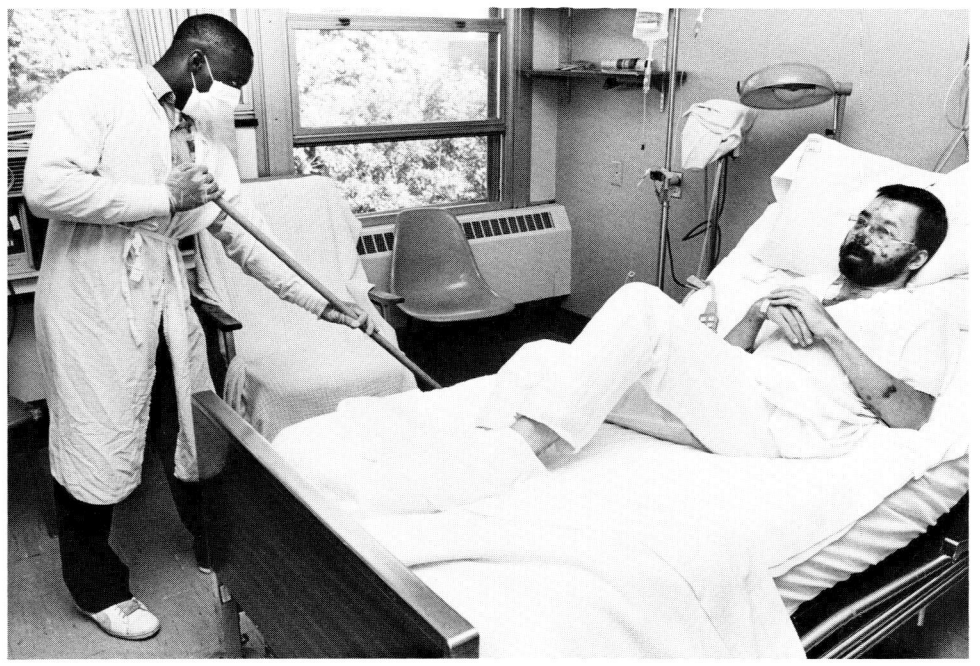

Stephen Jenteel was diagnosed as an AIDS victim in December 1984; six months later he was in a hospital bed at Upstate Medical Center, Syracuse, N.Y., where a hospital aide wears a mask, gloves, and gown to protect himself. Jenteel died in October.

BOB MAHONEY, SYRACUSE (N.Y.) NEWSPAPERS
JANET KNOTT, THE BOSTON GLOBE

Peter Lornardi, with the AIDS Action Committee, helps his friend, Fernando, who went to the Deaconess Hospital in Boston for treatment of the disease. Fernando died six weeks after this photograph was made.

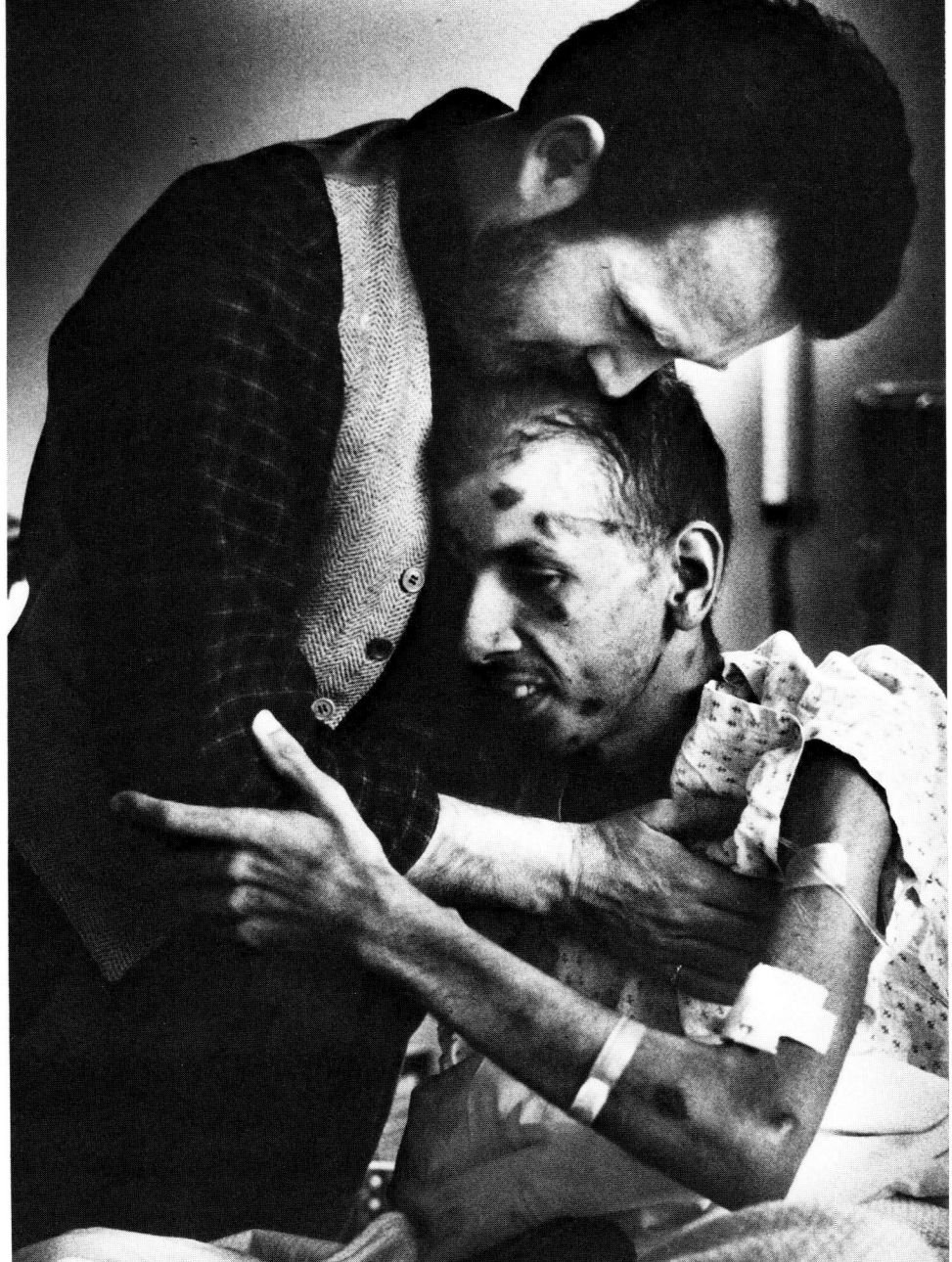

CRAIG LEE, THE SAN FRANCISCO EXAMINER
DAVID SCHREIBER, SAN BERNARDINO (CALIF.) SUN

Above, in San Francisco, people concerned with the lack of medical progress in AIDS cases hold a candlelight vigil near City Hall.

Right, in San Bernardino, family members mourn the death of a 12-year-old hemophiliac, who contracted AIDS through blood transfusions.

AIDS invasion

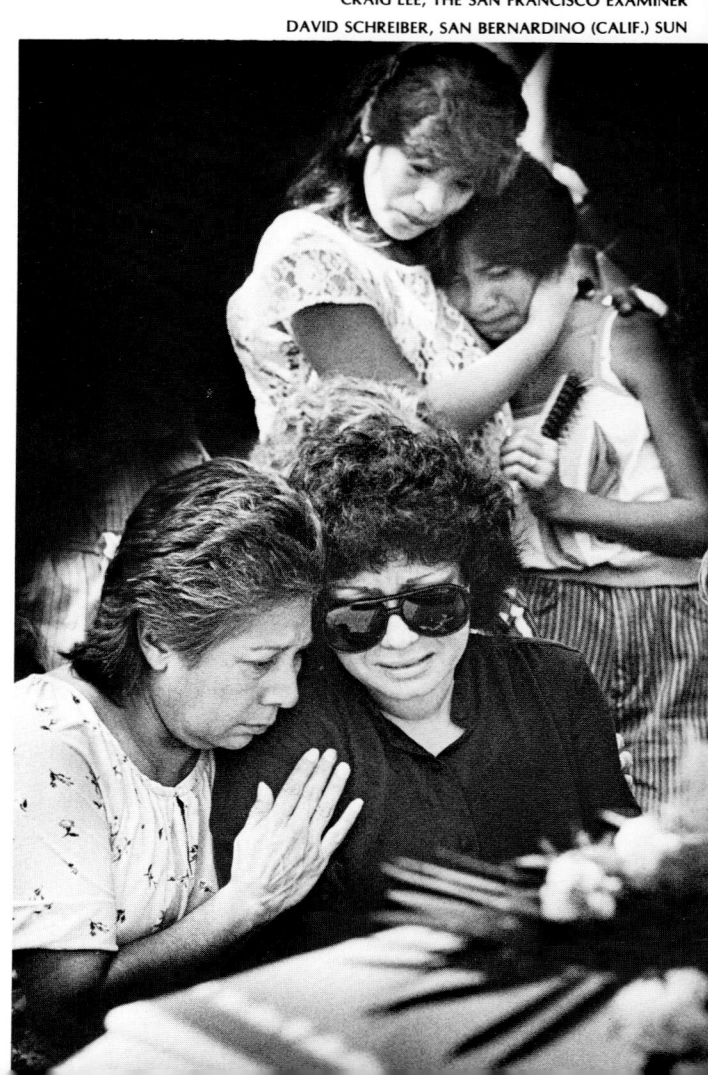

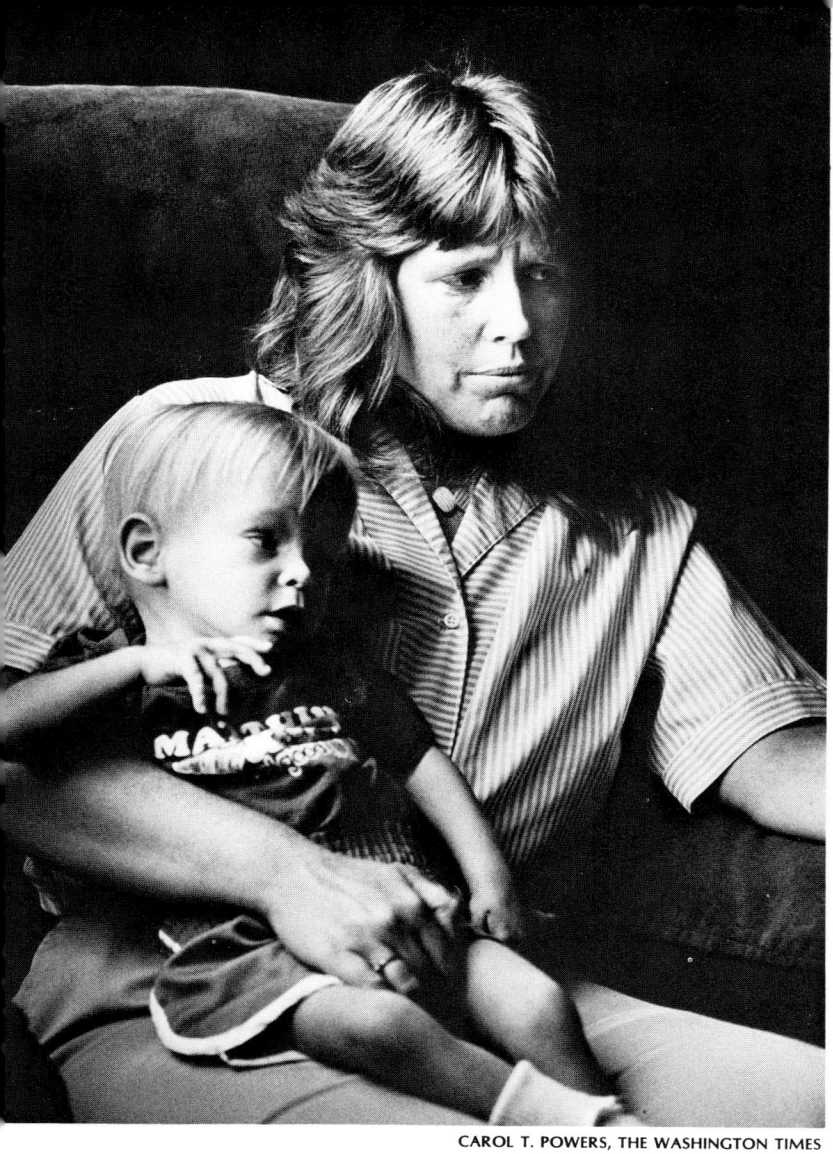

CAROL T. POWERS, THE WASHINGTON TIMES

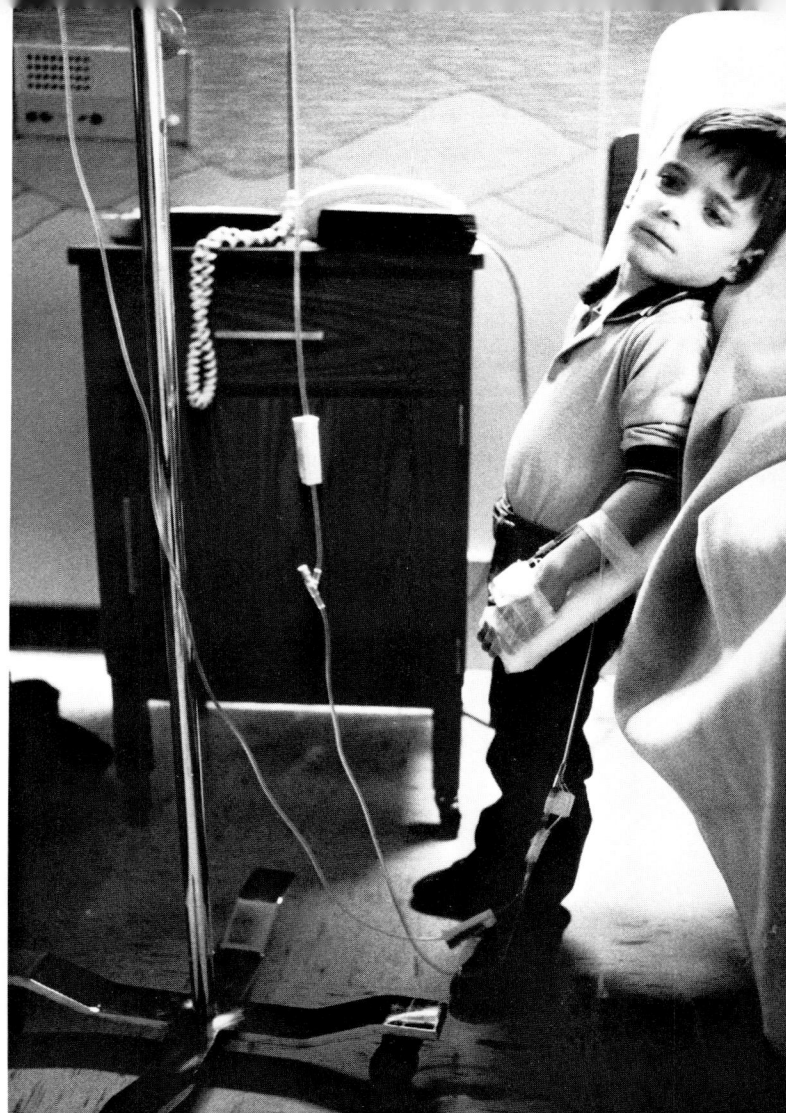

CHERYL NUSS, SAN JOSE (CALIF.) MERCURY NEWS

FREDERIC LARSON, THE SAN FRANCISCO CHRONICLE

Upper left, Suzan Kozup holds back her emotions in Washington, D.C, as she tells how son Matthew contracted AIDS from a blood transfusion just after he was born.

Above, in California, 4-year-old Matthew has AIDS. He's afraid that if he touches someone, they will die.

Left, a couple from a small California town lost their son to AIDS. Reported Photographer Frederic Larson: "He was a hemophiliac and young ... "

Canon Photo Essayist Award —
'A real sense of danger . . .'

By Marcia Prouse
Detroit Free Press

In Durban, South Africa, David C. Turnley, staff photographer for the Detroit Free Press, was taking pictures of the segregated beaches.

While photographing a sign at an all-white beach, Turnley, who is white, was confronted by a half dozen South African whites who threatened to smash his camera, called him a communist, and told him to leave the country. Later, after photographing a beach marked "For the black race only," he was detained by Indian police and told that he wasn't allowed there.

"The combination of those two experiences defined what the country is all about," Turnley says.

Turnley was the only American newspaper photographer still in South Africa in the final months of 1985. He worked with Free Press reporter Larry Olmstead.

Sweeping restrictions were imposed on journalists by the South African government Nov. 3. Given the small number of journalists left in the country at that time, "No one wants to be thrown out of the country for violating government restrictions for a relatively ordinary news story or picture, because to do so would further reduce the flow of information out of South Africa," Turnley says.

Turnley, 30, also was filing news pictures via Associated Press. Through an agreement with Black Star picture agency, his photographs also appeared in Time, Life, and other international publications.

"Being a journalist in South Africa is very difficult whether you are black or white, for all kinds of reasons," Turnley says. "It doesn't seem to matter what color you are — the media is either accepted or it's not."

Turnley has been detained three times by police. But dealing with them is only part of it.

"Almost every day, almost every time you go into a township, you feel a real sense of danger from both South Africans who are suspicious of the press and from the military police," he says.

David Turnley has worked at the Free Press since 1980. His identical twin, Peter, is a photographer for the Rapho picture agency in Paris and a contract photographer for Newsweek QS magazine. They both graduated from the University of Michigan in 1977 with bachelor's degrees in French, dropped out of school at different times for a year to study in France, and knew throughout their college careers that they wanted to be photojournalists.

Right, a man shouts "Amandla," which means "power," during a funeral for black unrest victims in Duncan Village, near East London.

Canon Essay

In mid-October, police in an armored truck raced toward a crowd of 1,000 angry persons in Athlone near Capetown. The mob broke and ran as police fired into the crowd. Police then chased the crowd, returning with a 17-year-old in custody. Despite the pleas of the youth's mother, the police loaded him into their truck and drove away.

In late August, a crowd gathered outside the stadium at Athlone, preparing to join the Rev. Allan Boesak in a protest march to Pollsmoor Prison, where Nelson Mandela was held. Police with bullwhips corralled the people, then charged. The incident sparked what became a continued period of unrest and violence in the West Cape area.

A suspected police informer is attacked at a funeral. Members of the angry crowd placed a tire filled with petrol — called a "necklace" — around the man's neck and were ready to light it when clergymen intervened.

Black youths demonstrate after setting tires and debris afire in Gugeletu Township.

Friends and family grieve over the body of a baby killed by South African police during an incident in Mamelodi Township. Funerals are the only legal reason that blacks may assemble, and thus are not only occasions for mourning but also forums for political and spiritual protest.

In silence, thousands of blacks raise their fists as pallbearers carrying bodies of unrest victims pass by on the way to a cemetery in Duncan Village near East London. The coffins are covered with United Democratic Front flags.

Canon Essay

Above, a black man picks up balls for bowlers at the exclusively white Durban Country Club.

Below, sisters walk home from a school in suburban Johannesburg with their nanny.

Above, even though the passenger seat is empty, farmhand William Gathie's place is in the back of a truck driven by Johan Richter. Richter's Afrikaner farm is in the Orange Free State, a large agricultural province where the effects of South Africa's apartheid system are most visible. Gathie works a six-day week, 12 hours a day, and earns the equivalent of $12 a month.

Left, a golfer at the white country club in Durban waits for an iron from his caddy. All service jobs at the club are held by blacks.

Canon Essay

Right, in her village hut in KwaHlongwa, south of Durban, ReJoyce Shozi boils water while feeding her son.

Below, Shozi's husband, Johannes — like thousands of blacks — had to leave his village home and migrate to a city to find work. Here he walks with his sons down a mountainside to his village, after making a two-hour train trip from Durban, where he works. Because of the cost and travel time, he sees his family only once a month.

Left, Protas Madlala, a South African, and Suzanne Leclerc, an American, were married in what is thought to be the first legal wedding between a white and non-white in South Africa after the government scrapped the Mixed Marriages Act. But because Madlala is black, they are not allowed to live in a city.

Desmond Tutu, Anglican bishop and Nobel Prize winner, hugs Winnie Mandela, wife of the imprisoned South African dissident and black leader Nelson Mandela, at her home in Soweto.

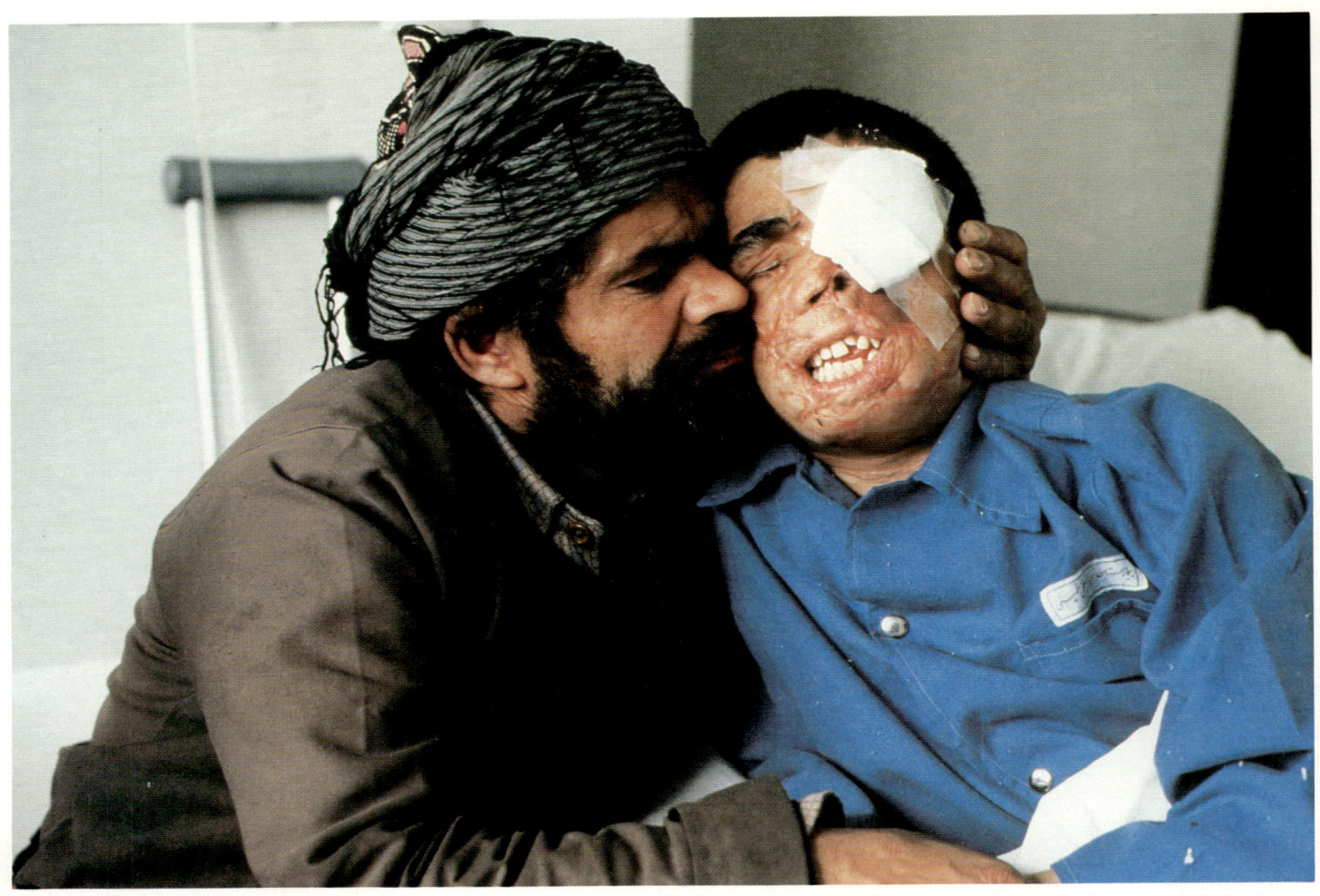

SECOND PLACE MAGAZINE PICTURE STORY, MICHAEL COYNE, NEWSWEEK (BOTH PHOTOS)

The photographs on this page are from Photographer Michael Coyne's reportage on life in Iran under the Ayatolla Khomeini. Above, a blind Kurdish shepherd who stepped on a mine is hugged by his father, who offered his eyes. But the boy was too badly injured for a transplant. Right, mullahs of the Faizeh Theological School in the holy city of Qom.

FIRST PLACE MAGAZINE PICTORIAL, COTTON COULSON, NATIONAL GEOGRAPHIC

SECOND PLACE MAGAZINE PICTORIAL, JAMES SUGAR, NATIONAL GEOGRAPHIC

Above, a thunderstorm threatens wheatfields west of Dodge City, Kan.

Left, fiery lava fountains spew from Hawaii's Kilauea volcano. A hyperactive vent for one of the earth's hot spots, Kilauea has erupted every few weeks for nearly three years.

Right, Quincy Jones and all-stars run through solos with Stevie Wonder, the world's most famous rehearsal pianist.

MAGAZINE PHOTOGRAPHER OF THE YEAR, HARRY BENSON, LIFE, (BOTH PAGES)

Historic Songfest for Africa

Life Photographer Harry Benson had an exclusive assignment one night in late January, when the nation's top recording stars got together to record "We Are The World."

Purpose: To help Africa's starving people.

In a chaotic, emotional session, the musicians produced a song that has raised millions for African relief.

And Benson had his story.

Above, Cyndi Lauper hits her mark.

Right, Willie Nelson and Michael Jackson exchange confidences.

Above, guards stand at attention as King Juan Carlos and Queen Sofia pose in Madrid's Palacio del Oriente.

Left, Queen Sofia, 47, vacations in Majorca with daughers Elena, 22, and Cristina, 20.

Spain's modern King

In the decade of his reign as the monarch of Spain, King Juan Carlos is credited with steering his country to democracy.

Today, reported Life Magazine, "He is hailed as a modern monarch who has led Spain into the world community."

Left, the king retrieves his retriever pups, Ajax and Atlas.

Above, a Yemeni Jewish bride near Gaza wears a wedding costume styled centuries ago, as Israel seeks to preserve the best of both its past and its high-tech present.

In Israel —
Transition

Photographer James Stanfield recorded what the National Geographic called Israel's current search for the center of a nation in transition.

Reported the Geographic: "In the past 15 years Israel has moved almost directly from an agricultural to a post-industrial economy," and called Israel a nation that "still lives in an uneasy fortress, surrounded by bitterness and threats ... But a new, unapologetic age stirs as Israelis return to the strength of their Jewish past."

MAGAZINE PHOTOGRAPHER OF THE YEAR, JAMES STANFIELD, NATIONAL GEOGRAPHIC (BOTH PAGES)

Above, embracing each other and their art, dancers of the Inbal troupe rehearse in Akko. The group achieves its identity through a meld of Yemeni and Jewish traditions.

Below, Rina Schenfeld, prominent Israeli modern dance artist, portrays "divine Presence."

Above, Pope John Paul II celebrates special sunrise mass for Czechoslovakians commemorating Saints Cyril and Methodius, ninth century pioneers of the Cyrillic alphabet.

Below, first snowfall in 14 years dusts worshippers leaving the Jan. 6 mass celebrating the Epiphany — the visit of the Magi to the Christ Child.

Above, inside St. Peter's Basilica, candidates for priesthood from 22 countries lie prostrate in humility as they take their vows during mass celebrated by Pope John Paul II.

Vatican City

Photographer James Stanfield made these photographs in the very human heart of a state raised to the glory of God — the world's smallest country, a sovereign enclave within the city of Rome, devoted to the spiritual guidance and temporal management of the world's largest congregation, the Roman Catholic Church.

45

Right, in Japan, the life of a geisha still requires hours of preparation on elaborate hair styles and stylized makeup before a "date": a men's dinner party where she will entertain with witty conversation and flirtations.

Below, in the Phillipines, guerrilla members of the New People's Army move through the jungle in a strike against government troops.

HONORABLE MENTION MAGAZINE DIVISION, JODI COBB, NATIONAL GEOGRAPHIC
HONORABLE MENTION MAGAZINE PICTURE STORY, WAYNE SOURCE, NEWSWEEK

SECOND PLACE NEWSPAPER PHOTOGRAPHER OF THE YEAR, JOHN KAPLAN, THE PITTSBURGH PRESS

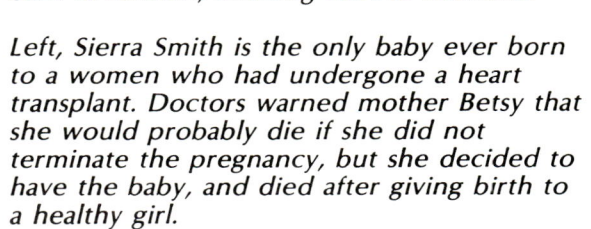

FIRST PLACE NEWSPAPER PICTORIAL, TED KIRK, JOURNAL-STAR NEWSPAPERS (LINCOLN, NEB.)

Above, freshly-painted feed wagons are arranged outside Nebraska State Fair dairy barn in Lincoln, awaiting start of activities.

Left, Sierra Smith is the only baby ever born to a women who had undergone a heart transplant. Doctors warned mother Betsy that she would probably die if she did not terminate the pregnancy, but she decided to have the baby, and died after giving birth to a healthy girl.

Those unfriendly skies

"A horrific year for air travel": That's how the Associated Press assessed 1985. Nearly 2,000 persons died in commercial air crashes.

Accidents were not the only horror in commercial air travel. Air terrorists were hard at work. The most dramatic hijacking came in June, when Shiite terrorists took over TWA Flight 847 en route from Athens to Rome.

The plane was ordered to Beirut, where hijackers shot a U.S. Navy enlisted man and demanded the release of comrades held in Israel.

The nightmare ended after 17 days. None of the terrorists involved was captured.

Below, one of the hijackers aboard TWA Flight 847 waves off a Shiite militiaman after he delivered newspapers to the sky pirates.

JAMAL SAIIDI, ASSOCIATED PRESS

BELOW, FIRST PLACE NEWSPAPER GENERAL NEWS, DENNIS COOK, ASSOCIATED PRESS

ISMAIL, AGENCE FRANCE-PRESSE

Above, TWA Pilot John Testrake answers journalists' questions under hijacker's gun.

Left, San Franciscan Victor Amburgy is welcomed home by niece Danelle Kruse after his release from Flight 847.

Below, relatives of Navy diver Robert Dean Stetham meet plane that brought his body home. Hijackers shot Stetham, dumped his body on the airport runway.

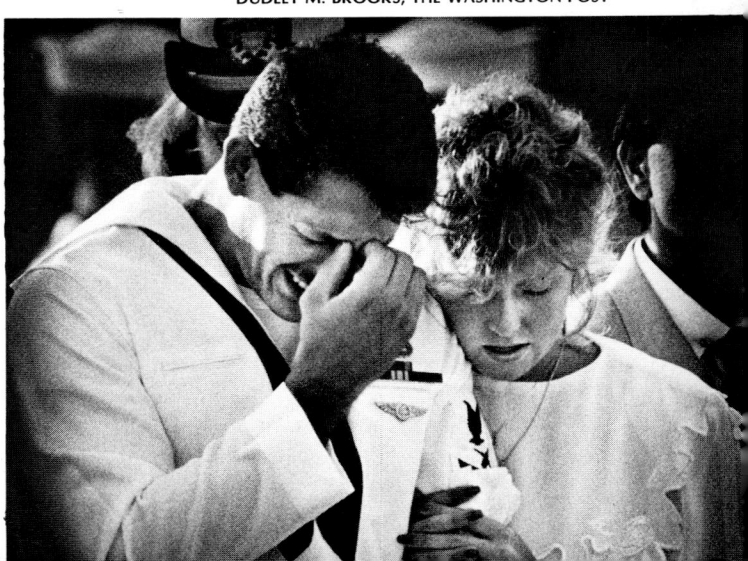

DUDLEY M. BROOKS, THE WASHINGTON POST

MAC
USAF
67953

Above, memorial services for the soldiers are held in a hangar at Ft. Campbell.

CHARLES STEINBRUNNER, DAYTON (OHIO) NEWSPAPERS, INC.

The 101st comes home

Worst tragedy in U.S. military air history came Dec. 12, 1985, when 248 soldiers based at Ft. Campbell, Ky., were killed; their Arrow Air jet went down after takeoff at Gander, Newfoundland.

Members of the 101st Airborne, the troops were on their way home from six months of duty on the Sinai Penninsula.

The tragedy plunged the entire nation into mourning.

Left, first bodies of the Gander crash victims arrive at Dover, Del., AFB.

LEFT, JOE SONGER, NASHVILLE (TENN.) BANNER

Right, President and Mrs. Reagan meet with each bereaved family to offer consolation after the service.

RIGHT, BILL LUSTER, THE COURIER-JOURNAL AND LOUISVILLE (KY.) TIMES

Death in Dallas

A Delta jet makes an approach to a runway at Dallas/Ft. Worth Airport as FAA officials inspect the tail section of Delta Flight 191, early in August. The L-1011 jet had been subjected to violent windshear in its final approach, causing it to bounce off an expressway and slam into a storage tank. The crash killed 133 persons aboard the plane.

MICHAEL DELANEY, THE MIAMI NEWS

520 died here

Rescue crews search the wreckage of a Japan Air Lines 747 in rugged terrain in central Japan after a mid-August accident.

A 12-year-old girl, Keiko Kawakami, was one of two persons who survived the JAL crash; 520 persons were killed when the jumbo jet went down.

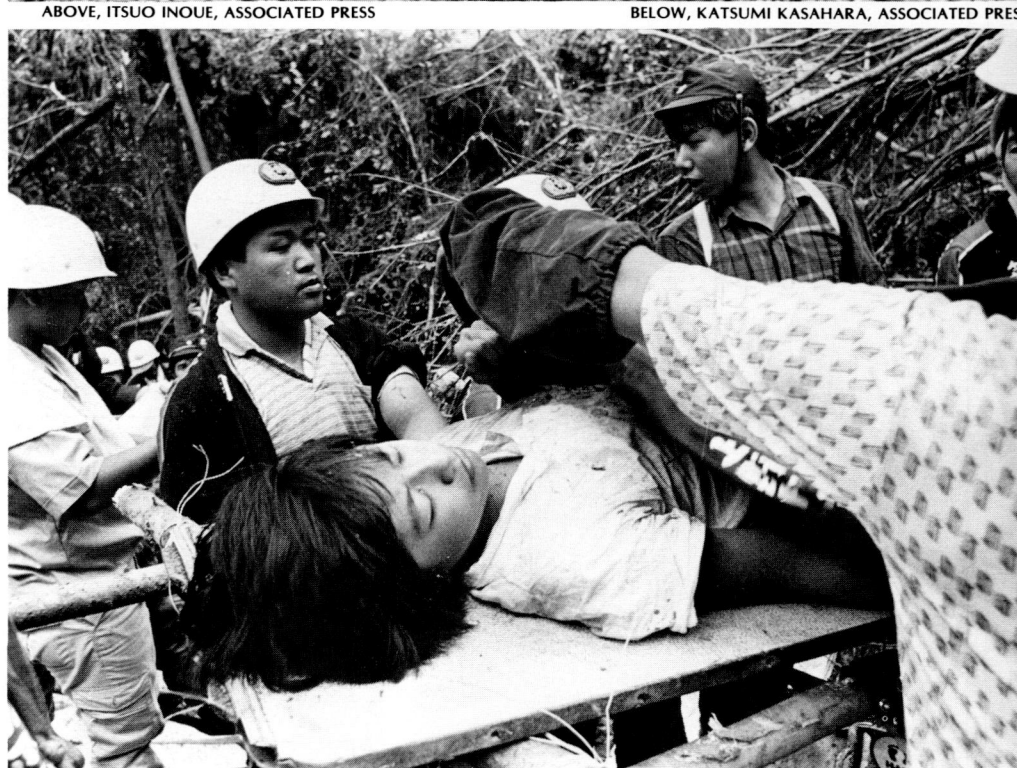

ABOVE, ITSUO INOUE, ASSOCIATED PRESS

BELOW, KATSUMI KASAHARA, ASSOCIATED PRESS

MARK HERTZBERG, THE RACINE (WIS.) JOURNAL TIMES

Above, three priests walk through the wreckage of a Midwest Airlines DC-9 that crashed after takeoff at Milwaukee's Mitchell Field in September, killing all 31 people aboard.

Left, an explosion rips out the cockpit of a Royal Jordanian ALIA Airline Boeing 727 at Beirut Airport in mid-June. Hijackers blew up the plane after releasing 48 passengers and nine crew members.

Midwest/Mid-East

HERVE MERLIAC, ASSOCIATED PRESS

MICHAEL S. WIRTZ, DALLAS TIMES HERALD

Above, as though the economic problems of farming aren't enough, this farmer watches a brush fire roll across his land in Brevard County, Fla.

Left, in Verdigre, Neb., 2-year-old Nathan, left, and 3-year-old Janet walk with their father, Stan Holan, on the family farm, which they are about to lose. It was a time when another farm went under every six minutes.

Crisis on the farm

Call it the biggest paradox of 1985: in a year when African famine victims drew continued attention, one of the biggest domestic news stories was the plight of the American farmer, whose bountiful harvests, said the Associated Press, "sank him even deeper in debt."

The tragedy of the American farmer did not come as a surprise. His economic troubles had been building since 1982, when both land prices and farm loan interest rates peaked out. Year by year since then, he has seen his productive flexibility slip away, eroded by high production costs and lackluster prices for his crops.

But in 1985, the rural drama became newsworthy, as farm activist groups banded together to save their neighbors, and as the problems of rural America became, increasingly, the concern of the rest of the nation.

Above, in Clinton County, Mo., Perry Wilson (white cap) is backed by 500 persons in a courthouse confrontation with sheriff's deputies and state troopers. They were fighting the sale of Wilson's farm at a foreclosure auction.

Below, in Gove, Kan., Clarence Bryant, an American Agriculture Movement supporter, protests to troopers because he wasn't allowed to bid on individual items at a forced sale of farm property. The sale went through.

FRANK NIEMEIR, THE KANSAS CITY (MO.) TIMES

CHARLIE RIEDEL, THE HAYS (KAN.) DAILY NEWS

THOMAS DODGE, FREELANCE (TRUMAN, MINN.)

DAVID ZALAZNIK, THE CEDAR RAPIDS (IOWA) GAZETTE

Above, highway patrolmen peer into the cab of a pickup containing the body of Iowa farmer Dale Burr, who committed suicide on a wintry country road after killing his wife, a neighbor, and the president of his bank. Reason: despondency over growing farm debts.

Left, these men were among some 600 farmers who shouted "No sale!" at a foreclosure auction of land owned by Jim Langman in Minnesota's Pope County. The protest stopped the sale. Langman subsequently re-negotiated his mortgage with the lender, saving his buildings and 22 acres of land.

Farm crisis spreads

59

MEL EVANS, OMAHA (NEB.) WORLD-HERALD, BOTH PHOTOS

Grim days . . .

Above, in Audubon, Iowa, a farm couple holds crosses in silent protest during bankruptcy hearing.

Below, beleaguered Nebraskans listen impassively to federal officials explaining their financial prospects.

60

Six miles of tractors move from Kismet, Kan., to Plains, Kan., in concert with a national farm demonstration: 240 farm implements being driven in a desperate attempt to draw attention to farmers' problems.

FRANK NIEMEIR, THE KANSAS CITY (MO.) TIMES

FRANK NIEMEIR, THE KANSAS CITY (MO.) TIMES
NANCY STONE, THE DAILY HERALD (ARLINGTON HEIGHTS, ILL.)

Above, responding to the American farmers' distress, country music acts and rock-and-roll stars performed for 14 hours during the Farm Aid Concert in Champaign, Ill., in September. About 80,000 persons attended.

Right, superstar Willie Nelson was a main force in producing Farm Aid Concert as well as performing during the event.

. . . and, a response

ART MERIPOL, ARKANSAS GAZETTE (LITTLE ROCK)

Joy of the Farm Aid Concert shines on the face of a young participant as he floats on a sea of hands over the crowd.

High water woes

Unsettled weather spawned major spot news stories in 1985, including floods that inundated a five-state area in the mid-Atlantic region. At least 48 persons were killed and 22,000 forced to evacuate their homes.

In West Virginia, Gov. Arch Moore mobilized the National Guard and asked President Reagan to designate 22 countries as disaster areas.

Right, in Fayette City, Pa., a volunteer fire captain, Charles Whitelaw, considers a nearly impossible task as the Monongahela River ebbs.

Below, two canoeists brave rushing waters of the Cheat River to inspect debris trapped by the Lake Lynn Dam on the Pennsylvania-West Virginia border.

BILL WADE, THE PITTSBURGH PRESS
ROBERT J. PAVUCHAK, THE PITTSBURGH PRESS

THOMAS J. HAWLEY, THE MONROE (MICH.) EVENING NEWS

Flooding caused problems in the Midwest, too. Above, Mr. and Mrs. Arvin DuVall, of Detroit Beach, Mich., take an aquatic route from their home after Lake Erie's wind-blown water threatened 100 family dwellings.

Below, city workers in Peoria, Ill., remove parking meters so they won't rust as the Illinois River went over flood stage in March.

RENEE C. BYER, THE PEORIA (ILL.) JOURNAL STAR

Tornadoes, too

In May, a series of tornadoes swept across northwest Pennsylvania. One of the towns hardest hit: Atlantic, population 2,000, which was almost wiped out. Right, one Atlantican offers a symbol of hope by raising a flag over a ruined residence.

In Niles, Ohio, Charles Lewis, right, surveys tornado damage from what was a bedroom in his parents' home. Seven persons died when a June tornado hit Niles.

LARRY C. PRICE, THE PHILADELPHIA INQUIRER
PATRICK REDDY, THE CINCINNATI POST

MARK DUNCAN, ASSOCIATED PRESS

Above, debris in residential section of Albion, Pa., shows the path of a tornado that hit June 1.

Below, fireman rest after sifting through rubble in western Pennsylvania's South Beaver Township, seeking survivors of five tornadoes that ripped through area.

WILLIAM E. LYONS, THE NEW CASTLE (PA.) NEWS

And hurricanes:
Elena

Right, in Florida, commercial fisherman Richard Rain bails out his boat after Hurricane Elena washed it ashore in September. Rain lives on the island of Cedar Key, which sustained millions of dollars in damage.

Below, in Tampa, residents move to safety along a flooded causeway as Hurricane Elena moves in.

BILL WAX, THE GAINESVILLE (FLA.) SUN
RAUL DeMOLINA FOR ASSOCIATED PRESS

MIKE EWEN, TALLAHASSEE (FLA.) DEMOCRAT

Above, Ronnie Seymour is comforted by her mother, Veronica Goodley, after seeing the damage Hurricane Elena caused Seymour's home near Carrabelle Beach, Fla.

Below, a volleyball net in the gym at St. Petersburg's Northeast High School serves as a clothes line for Floridians whose homes were flooded or cut off by high water from Tampa Bay during Hurricane Elena's reign.

FRED FOX, THE TAMPA (FLA.) TRIBUNE-TIMES

BONNIE K. WELLER, DELAWARE STATE NEWS (DOVER, DEL.)

DENNIS YONAN, FREELANCE FOR THE HARTFORD (CONN.) COURANT

As Hurricane Gloria worked up the East Coast in late September, people went out, just to see how it felt. Above, a man in Rehoboth Beach, Del., grips a pole for support.

Upper right, a curious resident of New Haven, Conn., is stopped in his tracks by Hurricane Gloria. Estimated wind speed: 90 mph.

Add hurricanes:
Gloria

Right, George Wilgocki and Eva Klemas cling to a street sign in Old Saybrook, Conn., as they experience Hurricane Gloria's force.

PAULA BRONSTEIN, THE HARTFORD (CONN.) COURANT

70

JOHN SHECKLER, STANDARD TIMES (NEW BEDFORD, MASS.)

In New Bedford, Mass., three men try to keep Hurricane Gloria from smashing their craft on the rocks on Pope's Island. They lost.

JOHN LONG, THE HARTFORD (CONN.) COURANT

At Mystic, Conn., the sign was superfluous, and Hurricane Gloria blew everything up on shore.

On Orient, Long Island, an unhappy owner of a Rolls Royce tries to get to his auto, barely visible beside the building at the end of the dock. Hurricane Gloria prevailed, however, and the car stayed where it was.

LEFT, JUDY AHRENS, THE SUFFOLK TIMES (GREENPORT, N.Y.)

CHUCK COOK, THE TIMES-PICAYUNE PUBLISHING CORP. (NEW ORLEANS, LA.)
BRYAN S. BERTEAUX, THE TIMES-PICAYUNE PUBLISHING CORP. (NEW ORLEANS, LA.)

Hurricane Juan occupied the attention of most residents of southern Louisiana late in October. Above, residents of a subdivision in Braithwaite, La., sandbag a levee to help protect their property from rising waters caused by the storm.

Right, thanks to Hurricane Juan, Claude Boudreaux bails water from his home near Houma, La.

Here comes Juan

ELIOT JAY SCHECHTER, NEWS/SUN-SENTINEL (FT. LAUDERDALE, FLA.)

And finally — Kate

Above, torn apart by Hurricane Kate, the sloop "Mai Hai" washes ashore. A Soviet ship rescued five persons from the storm waters.

Below, Mark and Lisa Stratton and son Marcus see what Hurricane Kate did to U.S. 98 near Eastpoint, Fla.

MAURICE RIVENBARK, ST. PETERSBURG (FLA.) TIMES (ORIGINAL IN COLOR)

The Philippines — Crisis in Paradise

At first flush the Philippines offer a visitor idyllic scenery, fertile rice fields and cheerful natives: a vacation paradise.

But in 1985, as its economy deteriorated and its people became increasingly restive, the Philippines became a nation in chaos. Death in the streets, guerrilla war, and prayers for the people missing at the hands of the Marcos regime replaced the seemingly serene lifestyle.

KAREN T. BORCHERS, SAN JOSE (CALIF.) MERCURY NEWS

SECOND PLACE NEWSPAPER PHOTOGRAPHER OF THE YEAR, JOHN KAPLAN, THE PITTSBURGH PRESS (BOTH PHOTOS)

Above, Filipino peasants re-vitalize their land by burning the husks of the rice that they harvest. Workers earn $2.50 a day.

Top picture, "Smoky Mountain," a garbage dump in Manila where poor people live in a squatter village and pick through trash looking for scraps of plastic, which earns them about 50 cents a day.

Bottom picture, student protestors rush a wounded comrade along a Manila street to a hospital. He lived.

Above, Philippine Army Rangers comb the jungle of Davao del Norte in search of New People's Army communist guerrillas.

Below, bodies of suspected communist sympathizers are stacked in a makeshift mortuary in the city of Davao. The Marcos regime is blamed for their deaths.

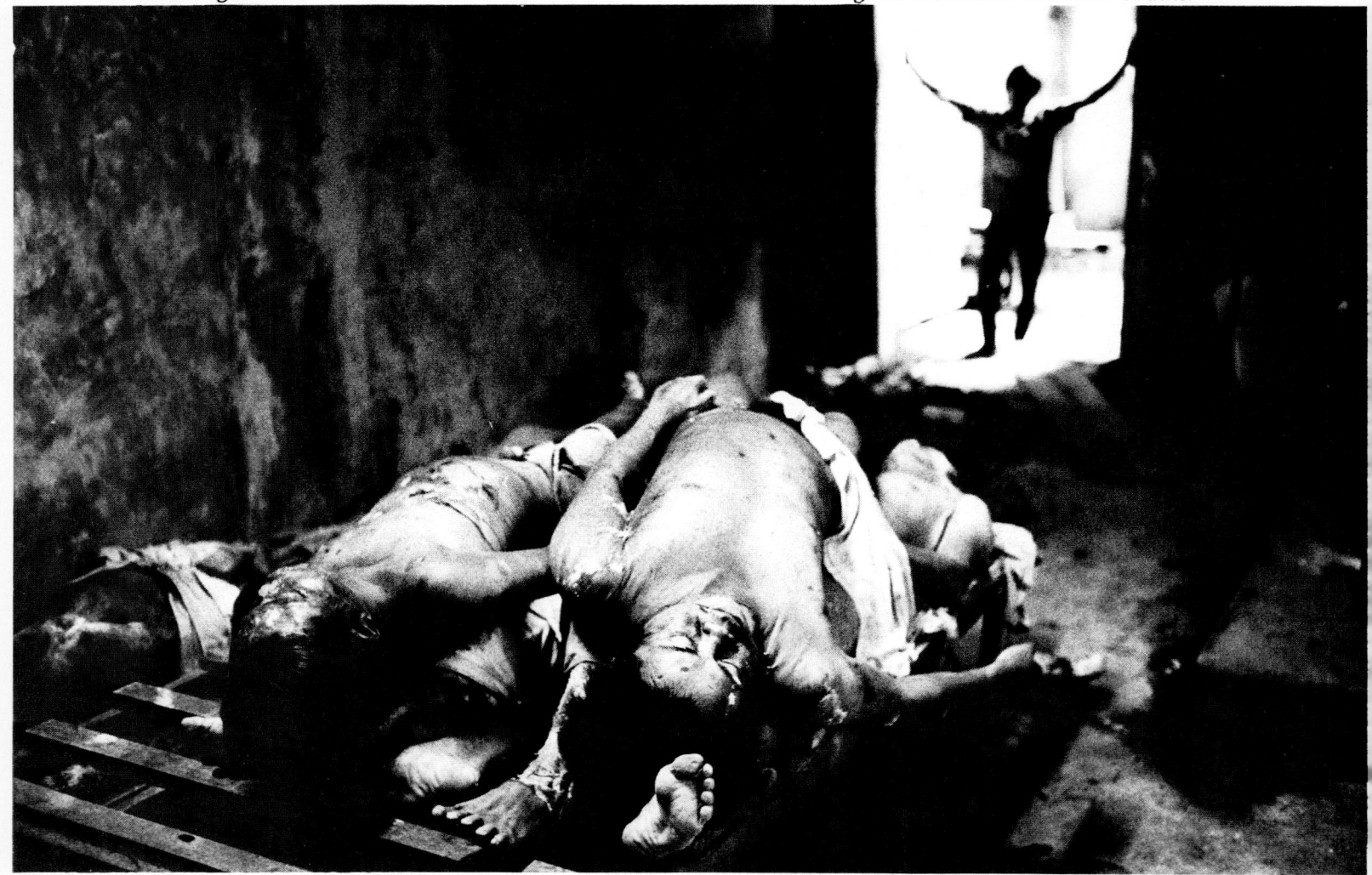

SECOND PLACE NEWSPAPER PHOTOGRAPHER OF THE YEAR, JOHN KAPLAN, THE PITTSBURGH PRESS (BOTH PAGES)

Despite increasing opposition, Philippines President Ferdinand Marcos showed no inclination either to step down or to change his policies. Above, at the convention where his candidacy for re-election was announced, Marcos gets a cooling hand from wife Imelda after a 45-minute campaign speech.

Left, opposition continues to mount as Corazon Aquino campaigns against Marcos in her home town of Tarlac. Bust in foreground is of her husband, Benigno, murdered in August 1983.

Crisis continues

DAVID HANDSCHUH, NEW YORK POST

Photographer David Handschuh got off four frames when a man in top hat and tails jumped off the Brooklyn Bridge. Suicide attempt? No — the subject wore a wet suit under his formal wear. He not only survived, but asked Handschuh for copies of the photograph.

THIRD PLACE NEWSPAPER SPOT NEWS, PIERRE GLEIZES, ASSOCIATED PRESS

Above, kidnapper Georges Courtois shoots at a crowd of journalists while running out of a high court in Nantes, France in December. He is chained to court president Dominique Baelhache. No one was injured; Courtois was retaken.

Below, in Oklahoma City an unidentified man falls to the ground, shot by members of an Oklahoma City SWAT team. He'd been holding a convenience store clerk hostage.

DAVID LONGSTREATH, ASSOCIATED PRESS

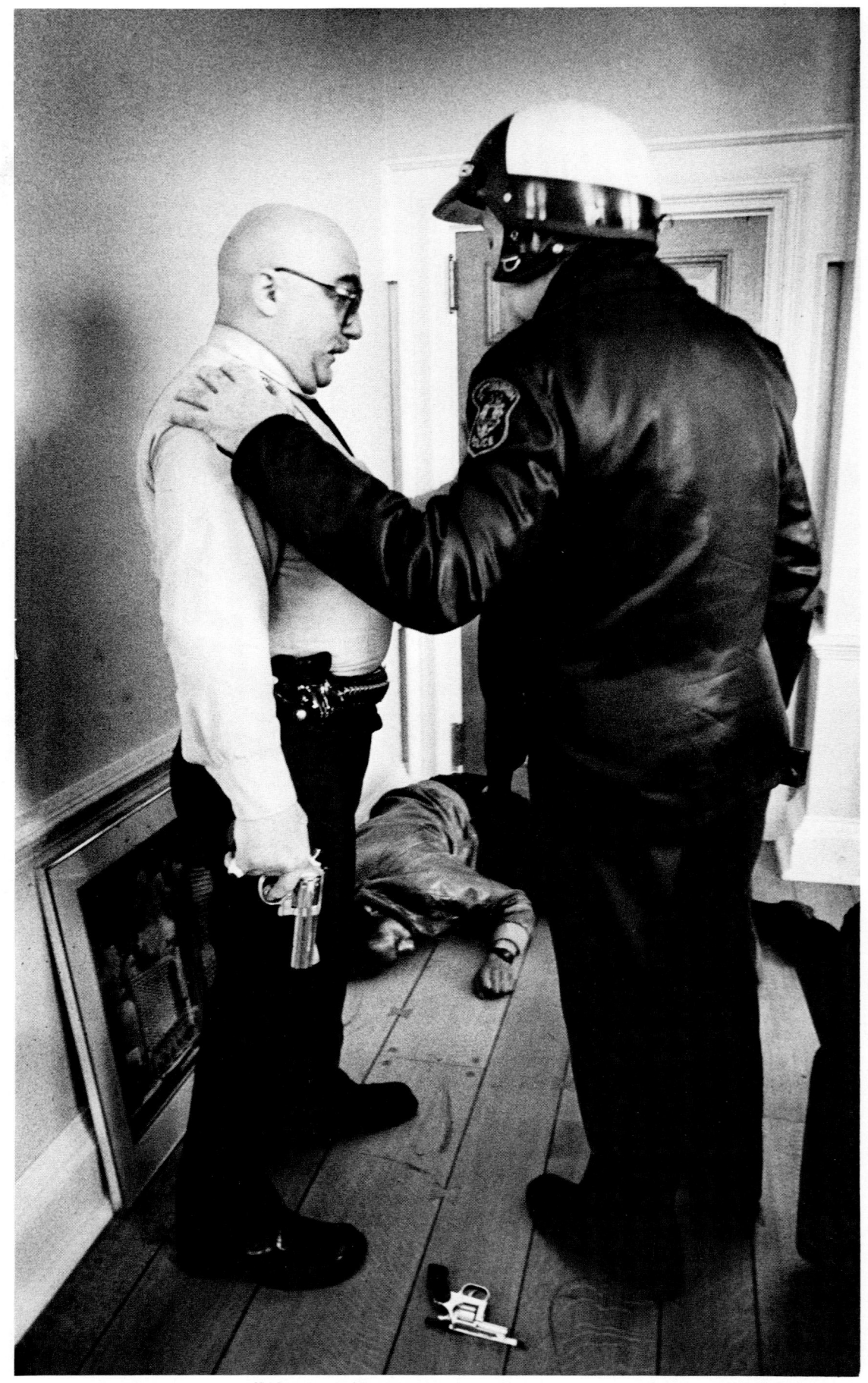

SECOND PLACE NEWSPAPER PHOTOGRAPHER OF THE YEAR, JOHN KAPLAN, THE PITTSBURGH PRESS

Fifteen seconds after fatally wounding a gunman in a downtown office building, Pittsburgh policeman Victor "Kojak" Balsamico is comforted by a fellow officer, Regis Bruegmann. Moments earlier, Rodland Jones had wounded his wife in her office, then hid in another room. Balsamico went after Jones, who turned his gun on the officer.

SECOND PLACE NEWSPAPER SPOT NEWS, DAVID PARKER, YUBA-SUTTER APPEAL-DEMOCRAT (MARYSVILLE, CALIF.)

A SWAT team member in Yuba City, Calif., races to safety with a 7-year-old boy, one of four children held hostage for four hours by their father. All children were eventually rescued without injury.

NEWSPAPER PHOTOGRAPHER OF THE YEAR STEVE RINGMAN, SAN FRANCISCO CHRONICLE

Above, accused of stealing property at gunpoint, two suspects find themselves looking down the wrong end of the barrel in San Francisco.

Below, in Santa Ana, Calif., a police officer responds to a silent alarm, and waits to see if anyone's inside a closed gun shop. There was. He was arrested.

GLENN KOENIG, LOS ANGELES TIMES

82

New England police officers, 5,000 strong, pay final respects to slain Patrolman Alain J. Beauregard, who was gunned down in Springfield, Mass., in the line of duty.

DAN GOULD, THE WORCESTER (MASS.) TELEGRAM

Goodbye, friend

Police Officer Alan Keith was writing a traffic ticket near the Blue Hills Reservation in Milton, Mass., when a speeding car clipped Keith's horse, Tivoli.

The impact threw the policeman and fatally injured his four-legged companion of three years.

Keith embraced his injured friend, then was helped away by fellow officers as Tivoli was put down.

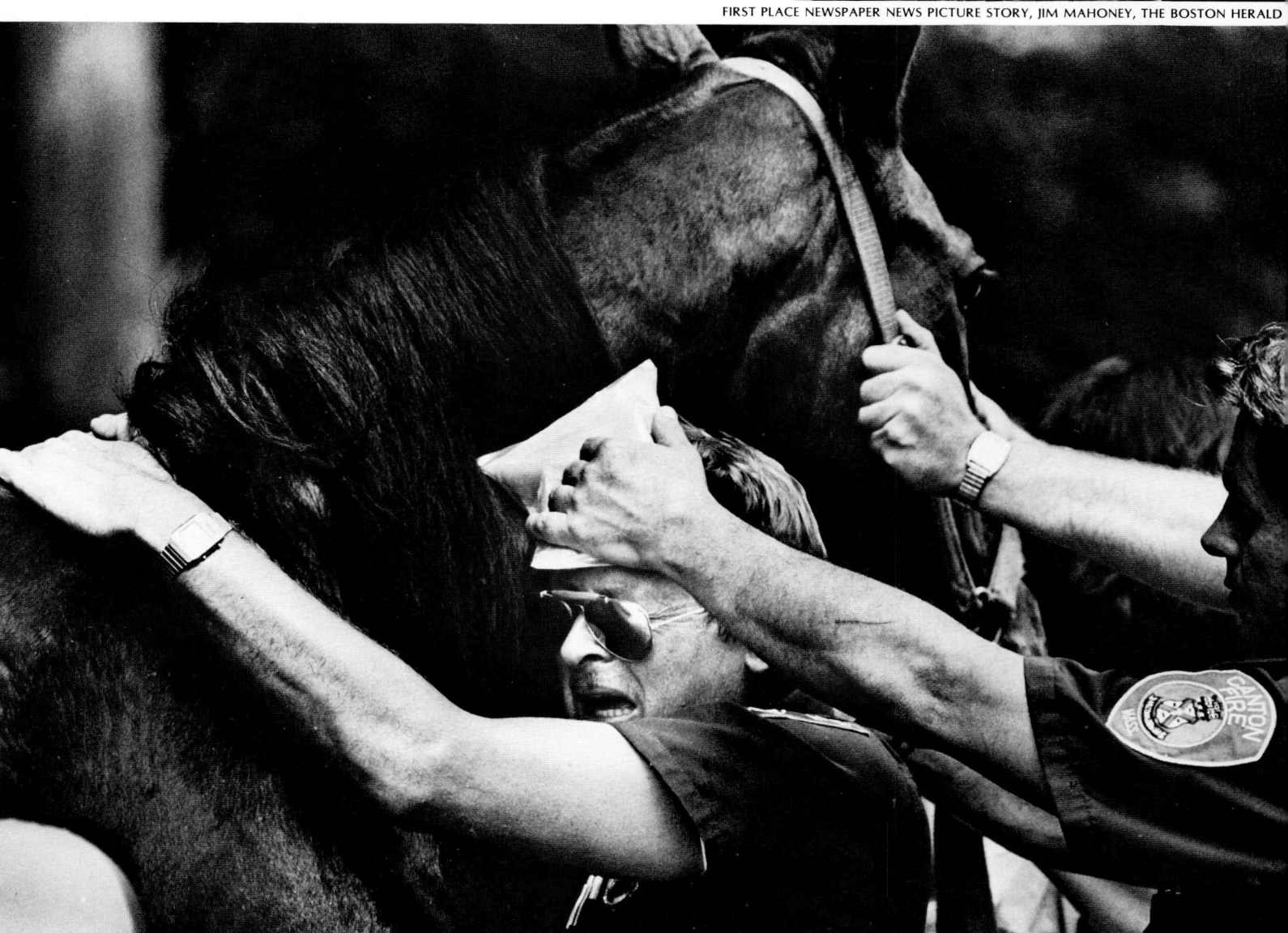

FIRST PLACE NEWSPAPER NEWS PICTURE STORY, JIM MAHONEY, THE BOSTON HERALD

85

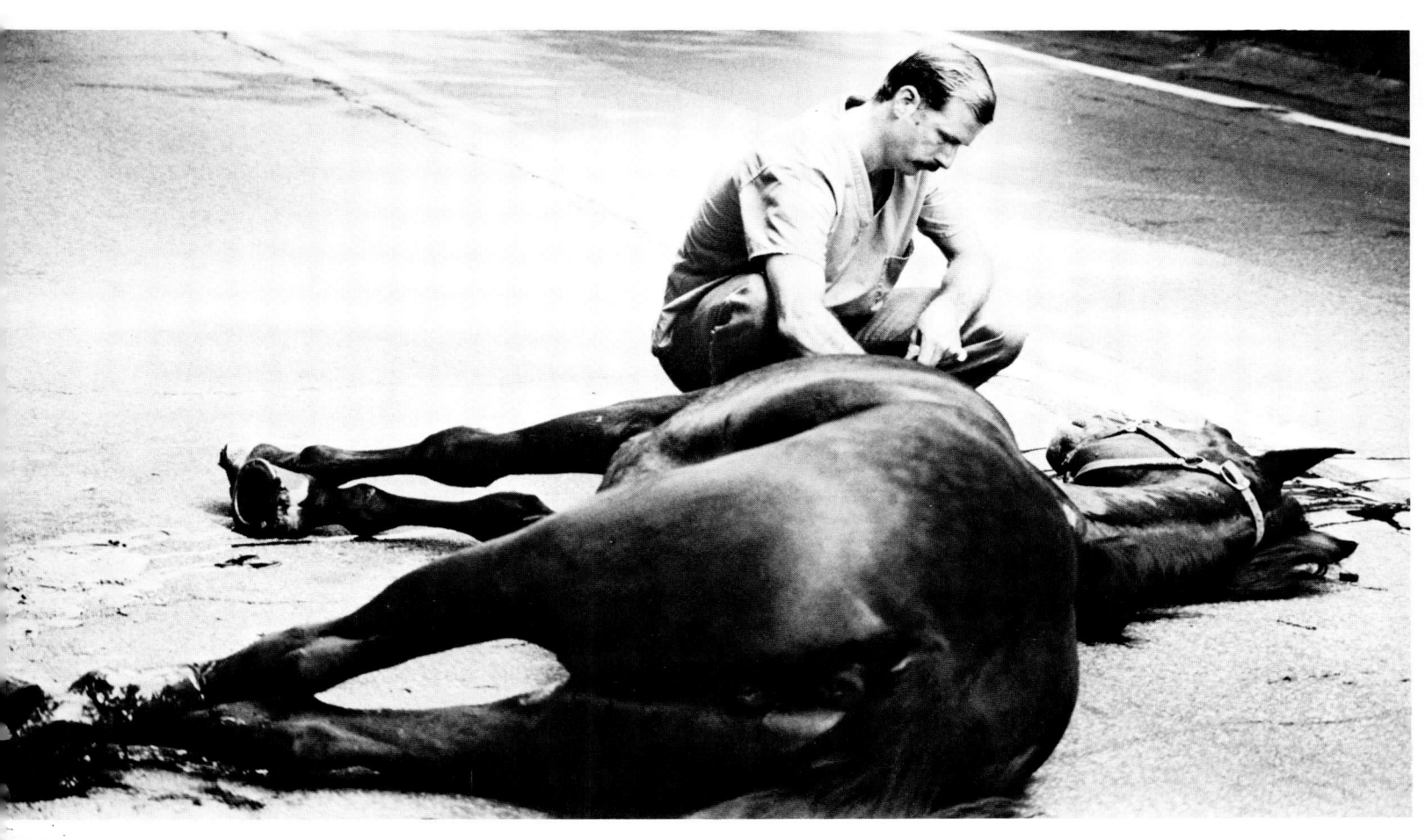

Above, during happier times in Oregon, the guru's followers bliss out over their leader during one of his "drive-by" appearances.

KURT E. SMITH, SEATTLE POST-INTELLIGENCER
HARLEY SOLTES, THE SEATTLE TIMES

Odyssey in Oregon

Bhagwan Shree Rajneesh called the wide-open spaces of central Oregon home for four years. But in November the cult leader wound up in jail in Charlotte, N.C., on charges of immigration fraud.

Rajneesh was returned to Oregon, where he pleaded guilty to two of 35 counts, paid a $400,000 fine, and was allowed to go back to his native India.

All that was left on Rajneesh's 64,000-acre hideaway were about 100 of his 5,000 followers, who prepared to liquidate the holdings and pay off some $35 million in debts.

Right, Rajneesh is guarded by a follower with an Uzi submachine gun as the guru appears before the faithful.

Left, in chains, Rajneesh is led into federal court in Charlotte, N.C. Two weeks later he was deported.

Below, alone in Rajneesh's temple in Oregon, two disciples embrace and consider a future without their guru.

HARLEY SOLTES, THE SEATTLE TIMES

CASEY MADISON, THE COLUMBIAN (VANCOUVER, WASH.)

SECOND PLACE NEWSPAPER GENERAL NEWS, DENNIS COOK, ASSOCIATED PRESS

In July, President Ronald Reagan gives the OK sign from the window of his hospital room at the Naval Medical Center, Bethesda, Md. He was recovering from surgery to remove a cancerous polyp from his intestines.

LARRY MORRIS, THE WASHINGTON POST

In August, President Reagan, in his first meeting with reporters since the July operation, points to where a growth diagnosed as a minor skin cancer was removed.

Just fine, thanks

DENNIS PAQUIN, UNITED PRESS INTERNATIONAL

Glad to be here

In Geneva, President Reagan and Soviet leader Mikhail Gorbachev exchange laughs at the beginning of their final summit ceremony in late November.

In West Palm Beach, 7-year-old Tara Sansbury offers a bouquet to Britain's Princess Diana as she and Prince Charles arrive in mid-November.

SHERMAN ZENT, THE PALM BEACH POST (WEST PALM BEACH, FLA.)

Right, anguished sendoffs are a regular occurrence at Tan Son Nhut airport outside Ho Chi Minh City in Vietnam. Once a month, some 300 Vietnamese board a plane to Bangkok as part of the U.N.-sanctioned Orderly Departure program. And at the airport are hundreds of people, straining for one last look at friends and relatives most won't see again.

Below, Ines Guadalupe (arm upraised) is reunited with her father, Salvadoran President Napoleon Duarte (center), after she was freed in Fantasma, east of San Salvador, by insurgents who kidnapped her and a friend early in September.

RICKY McKAY, COX NEWSPAPERS (WASHINGTON, D.C.)

IVAN MONTESINOS, AGENCE FRANCE-PRESSE

Above, Marilyn Klinghoffer kisses the coffin of her husband on its arrival in New York. Leon Klinghoffer was slain by hijackers aboard the Italian cruise ship Achille Lauro in October.

Below, an Air Force honor guard escorts the remains of nine Americans brought home — after a decade — from Vietnam.

RICHARD L. HARBUS, UNITED PRESS INTERNATIONAL

THIRD PLACE NEWSPAPER PHOTOGRAPHER OF THE YEAR, ERIC LUSE, SAN FRANCISCO CHRONICLE

DIETER ENDLICHER, ASSOCIATED PRESS
GARY WEBER, AGENCE FRANCE-PRESSE

Above, some 35 coffins are placed in a common grave in Tereso, Italy, the final resting place of some of the 232 victims of a dam disaster in the Dolomites in late July.

Right, Yevgeny Vtyurin, counsel for the Soviet Embassy in Washington, D.C., gives the "okay" signal when asked about Soviet sailor Miroslav Medvid, who twice jumped ship at Reserve, La. Vtyurin was aboard the grain-hauling Russian vessel, which was detained for about two weeks. It finally sailed, apparently with the some-time defector still aboard.

BOB RINGHAM, THE CHICAGO SUN-TIMES

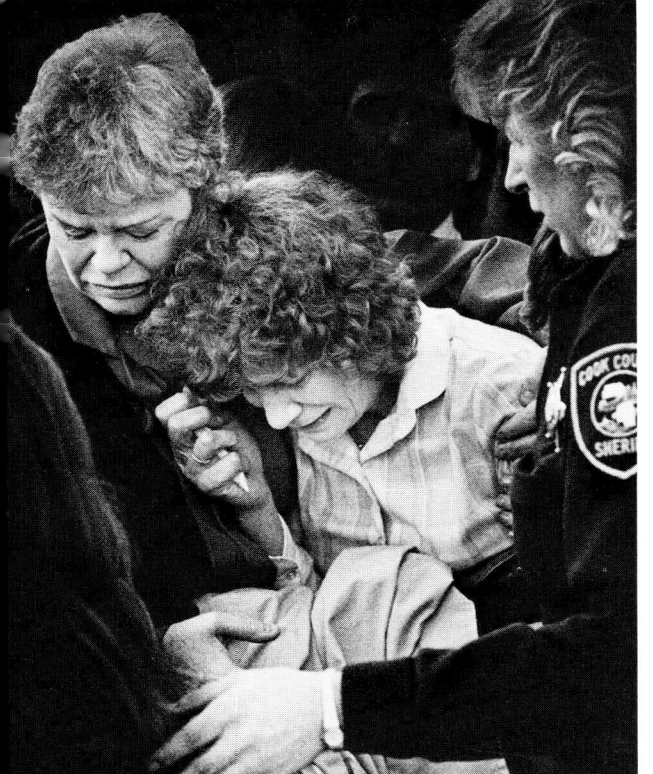

JIM KLEPITSCH, THE CHICAGO SUN-TIMES

In Illinois, the media followed the progress of prisoner Gary Dotson. He was released from jail when Cathleen Webb, who had accused him of rape seven years earlier, recanted that accusation. Above, Dotson faces the press after his release. Left, Dotson's mother is comforted after one court hearing on the matter.

93

Mom Doss carries on

In a cramped, inner-city apartment in West Philadelphia, an 8-year-old Cambodian girl named Mom Doss tried to keep her world from falling apart.

The youngster's family had been in this country three years when gastric cancer struck her mother. The tragedy forced the girl to become — at least for a few months — her own mother's mother, and the person who kept the family together.

When Mom's mother died, the girl's emotional roller coaster intensified. But while Mom slowly recovered, her father did not. Determined to salvage his life, he moved the family to the West Coast for a new beginning. It didn't work. At last report they had returned to West Philadelphia.

Below, Mom Doss tries to tease a smile from her dying mother.

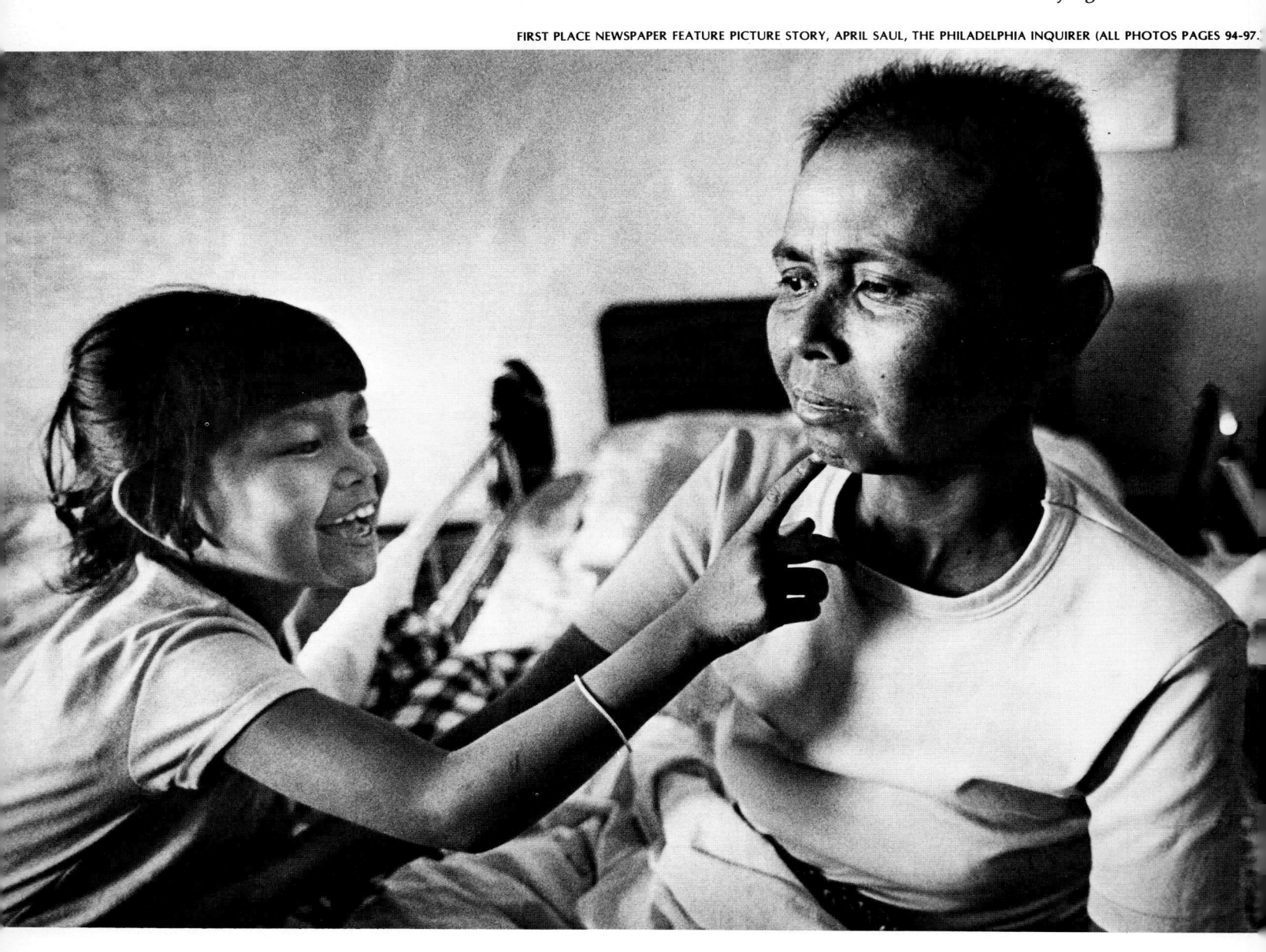

FIRST PLACE NEWSPAPER FEATURE PICTURE STORY, APRIL SAUL, THE PHILADELPHIA INQUIRER (ALL PHOTOS PAGES 94-97.

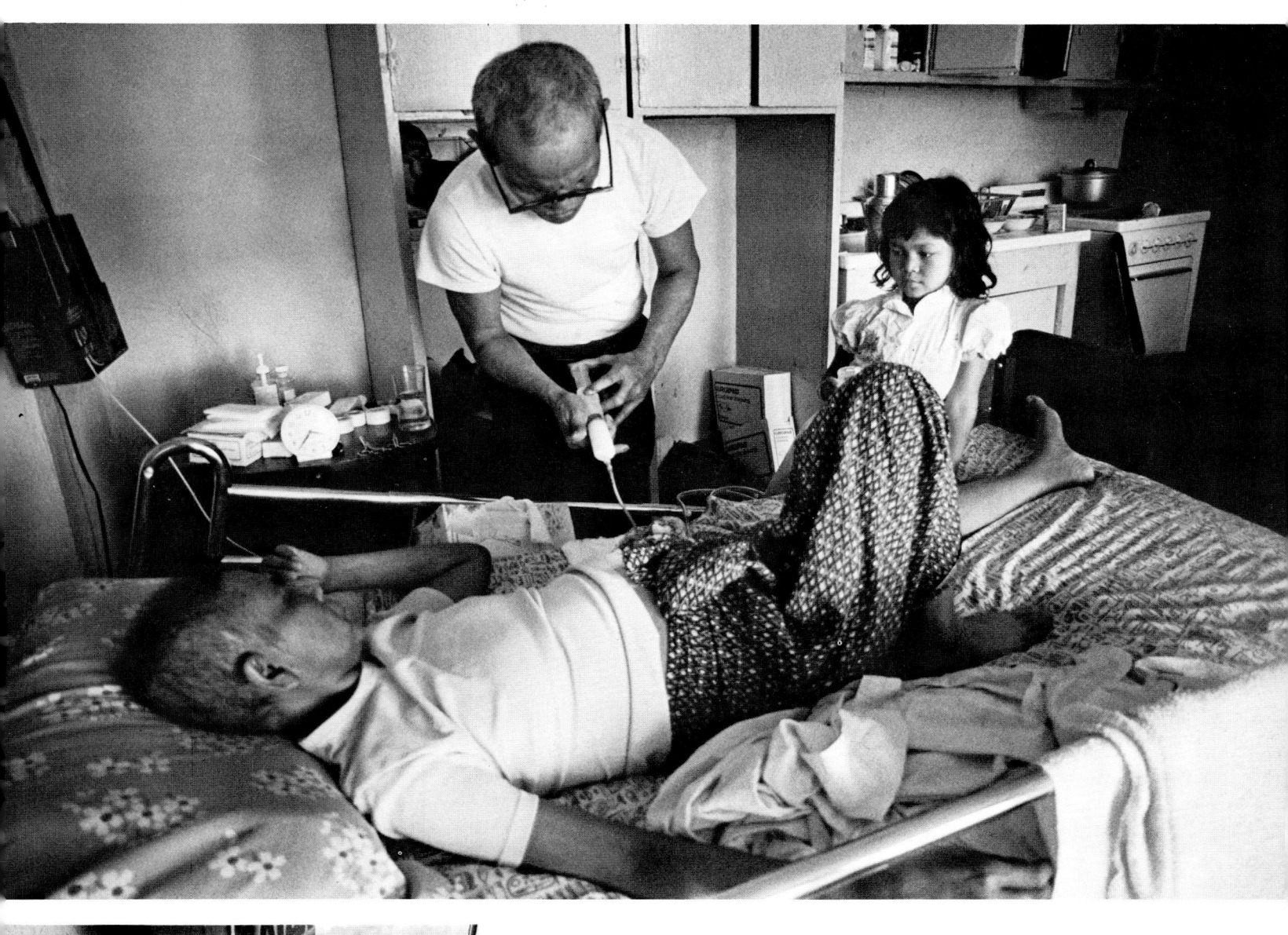

Above, Mom Doss and her father care for Mom's dying mother at home. Since her father spoke no English, Mom kept hospice workers apprised of her mother's condition. Left, Mom cleans a bedpan. Below, the girl uses a chair to reach the sink to wash dishes.

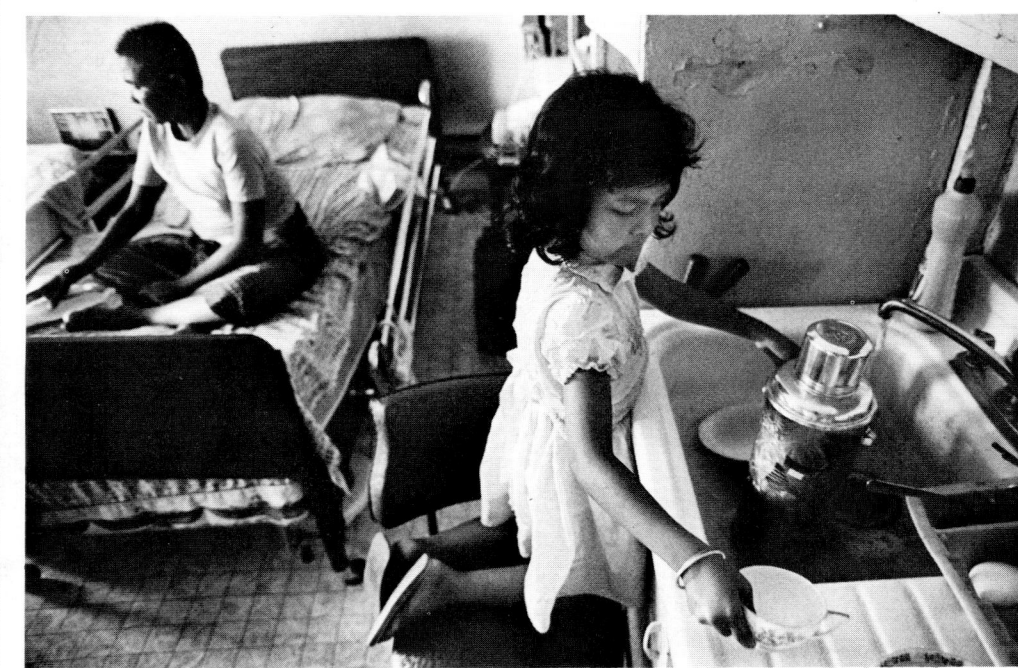

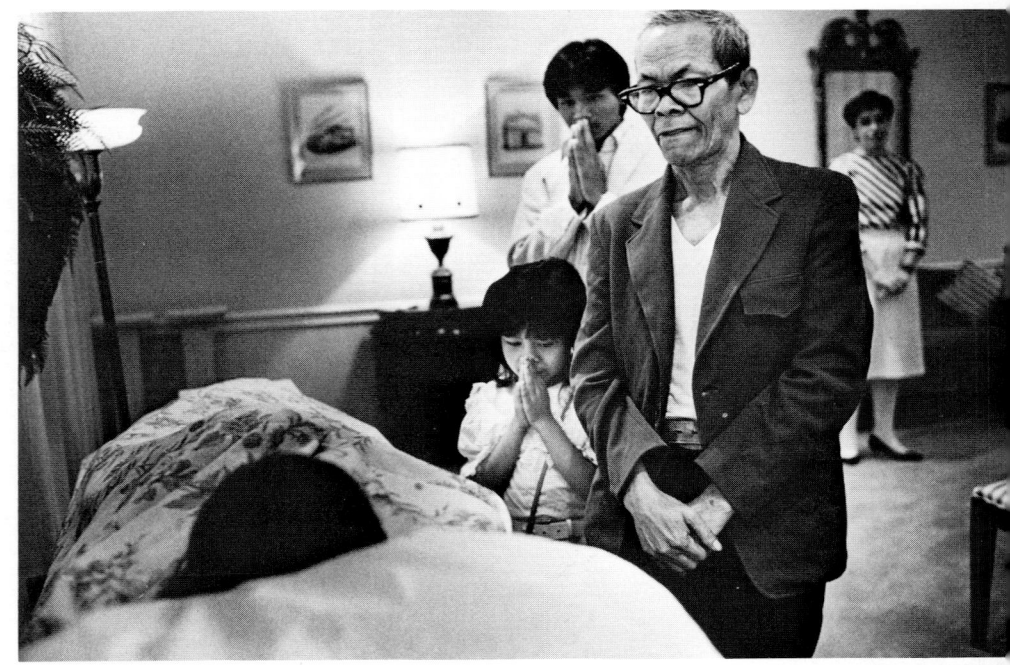

Mom's agony

At her mother's funeral, Mom joins her father and half-brother at the coffin.

During funeral service, Mom hugs an old pocketbook of her mother's, and quietly cries.

Above, Mom's teacher and classmates try to be understanding as the youngster deals with her grief.

Below, Mom waits as her father loads family possessions into a taxi, bound for the bus station and the West Coast.

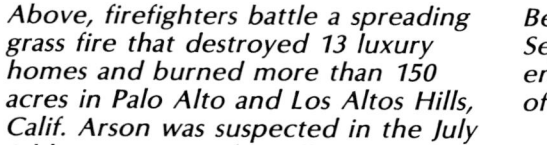

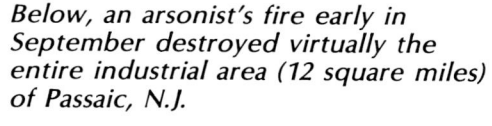

SAM FORENCICH, THE PENINSULA TIMES TRIBUNE (PALO ALTO, CALIF.)

Above, firefighters battle a spreading grass fire that destroyed 13 luxury homes and burned more than 150 acres in Palo Alto and Los Altos Hills, Calif. Arson was suspected in the July 2 blaze. Damage: $9 million.

Below, an arsonist's fire early in September destroyed virtually the entire industrial area (12 square miles) of Passaic, N.J.

JOHN BADMAN, ALTON (ILL.) TELEGRAPH

Above, smoke and flames envelop Shell Oil Co.'s Wood River complex in Roxana, Ill. The January explosion left one dead, seven injured.

NICK KELSH, THE PHILADEPHIA INQUIRER

It's always news

There's one spot news situation that every news photographer breaks in on: fire.

And 1985 provided this quintessential local story in abundance across the country.

LARRY STEAGALL, THE BREMERTON (WASH.) SUN

JOHN DZIEKAN, CHICAGO TRIBUNE

Above, only a photograph could capture the emotions displayed by firefighter Tammy Corcoran as fire destroys the John Elterich family home in Bremerton, Wash.

Left, four persons died in this mid-winter blaze in Chicago, including a child who apparently returned to the building to help relatives escape.

... and more fires

Right, Chicago firefighters cluster around the body of one of three comrades killed in a February fire in northwest Chicago. The cause: arson.

Below, Louisville firefighter Fred Mercer lends support to Craig Stevens in fighting a four-hour blaze at a tire storage site. Four youngsters, ages 10 to 13, were charged with second degree arson in connection with the fire, which sent black toxic smoke billowing over Louisville's skyline.

TOM CRUZE, CHICAGO SUN-TIMES
PAT McDONOGH, THE COURIER-JOURNAL AND LOUISVILLE (KY.) TIMES

Above, residents of Golden Gate, Fla., watch as flames destroy trees and brush across a canal from their homes. Brush fires burned across 20,000 acres in southwest Florida before the rainy season made a late appearance.

ERIC STRACHAN, NAPLES (FLA.) DAILY NEWS

Below, badly burned but purring loudly, this cat waited for her owners to return after a devastating forest fire in Los Gatos, Calif. She was taken to an animal hospital.

THIRD PLACE NEWSPAPER PHOTOGRAPHER OF THE YEAR, ERIC LUSE, SAN FRANCISCO CHRONICLE

A utility worker tries to shut off a fire hydrant after a car went out of control in Mar Vista, Calif.

After their car smashed into a tree in Chesapeake, Va., Christine Respess, 16, hugs her younger brother, Bryan, whose twin, Ryan, clasps his hands in prayer. The children were waiting for word of a fourth passenger, Christine McDowell, 17, still pinned in the car. McDowell sustained a mild concussion.

DEBRA MYRENT, FREELANCE, (CULVER CITY, CALIF.)
LOIS BERNSTEIN, THE VIRGINIAN-PILOT AND THE LEDGER-STAR (NORFOLK, VA.)

Swift, high water of Kings River swirls over a car that crashed in Sequoia National Park in California. Body of the driver remained in the vehicle more than two weeks before it could be salvaged.

ROBERT E. DURELL, THE FRESNO (CALIF.) BEE
BRYAN S. BERTEAUX, THE TIMES-PICAYUNE PUBLISHING CORP. (NEW ORLEANS, LA.)

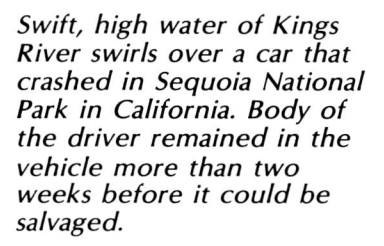

The cab of a tractor-trailer dangles over the railings of Interstate 10 in New Orleans after a rush-hour accident. The driver jumped about 25 feet to the roadway below.

Right, victims of a Palestinian terrorist attack in late December are sprawled in lounge area of Rome's Leonardo da Vinci Airport.

Below, U.S. marshals and Washington, D.C., police level guns at fugitives caught in a sting operation. The ruse netted almost 100 persons wanted for crimes ranging from murder and rape to narcotics law violations.

BRUNO MOSCONI, ASSOCIATED PRESS
BERNIE BOSTON, LOS ANGELES TIMES

'Dance of death'

Japanese dancer Yoshiyuki Takada fell 50 feet to his death while performing before hundreds of stunned spectators in downtown Seattle, Wash., early in September. He was one of four men featured in a "dance of life and death" while hanging from ropes from a six-story building. At left, the rope holding Takada breaks; below, a doctor tries vainly to revive the injured dancer.

GARY D. STEWART, ASSOCIATED PRESS
SHERRY BOCKWINKEL, BELLEVUE (WASH.) JOURNAL-AMERICAN

TOM VAN DYKE, SAN JOSE (CALIF.) MERCURY NEWS

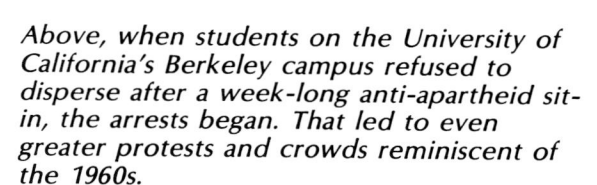

Above, when students on the University of California's Berkeley campus refused to disperse after a week-long anti-apartheid sit-in, the arrests began. That led to even greater protests and crowds reminiscent of the 1960s.

SKIP WEISENBURGER, THE MIDDLETOWN (CONN.) PRES

Above, campus security officers in Middletown, Conn., drag one of 130 protestors from the steps of Wesleyan University's administration building. The students were demonstrating against the school's South African investment policies.

Right, they called him "Night Stalker": Richard Ramirez, who was charged with 14 slayings and 36 other felonies that terrorized residents of Los Angeles and Orange County. On his way to arraignment, he displays Satanic markings on his hand: three sixes and a pentagram.

RIGHT, MICHAEL GOULDING, LOS ANGELES DAILY NEWS

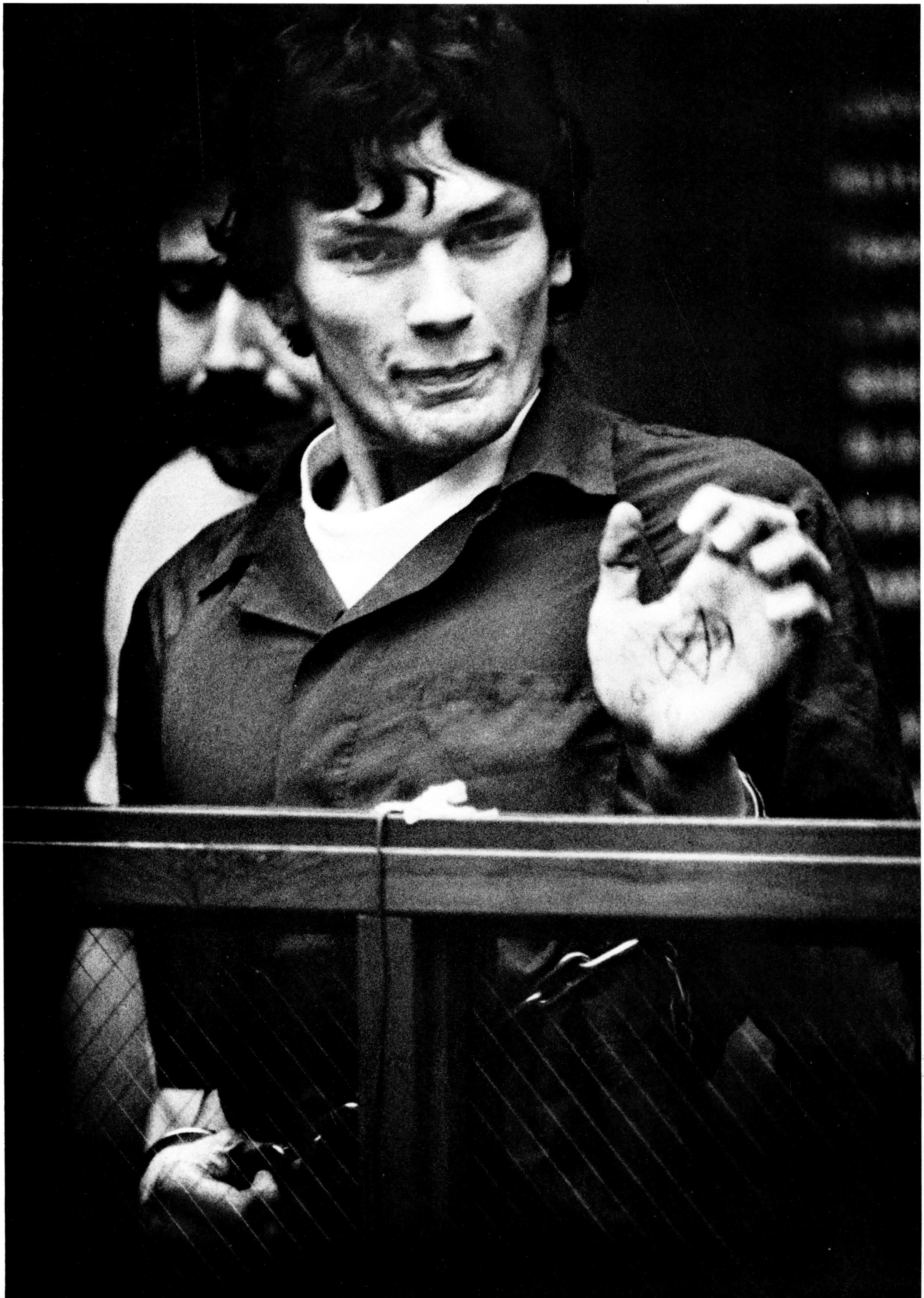

MARC CLERY, THE MIAMI HERALD

The Renegade Reef, a 26-year-old Dutch coaster abandoned in Florida's Miami River in 1981, went up in an 80-foot cloud of smoke after officials loaded her with 100 pounds of dynamite. The freighter sank off the Pompano Beach pier, becoming one more artificial reef.

SHERMAN ZENT, THE PALM BEACH POST (WEST PALM BEACH, FLA.)

More than 500 pleasure boats accompanied the tired Mercedes I out to sea in late March, where 360 pounds of TNT sank the hulk off Fort Lauderdale. The Venezuelan freighter had been grounded for 104 days on the waterfront property of Palm Beach socialite Molly Wilcox. It took Florida legislative action (and cash) to dispose of the abandoned vessel.

MILAN CHUCKOVITCH, THE COLUMBIAN, VANCOUVER, WASH.
REGINALD PEARMAN, THE TRIBUNE, OAKLAND, CALIF.

Above, when snow stopped traffic on the I-5 bridge between Vancouver and Portland, Tom Hepner of Vancouver took advantage of the delay to put on his snow tires.

Right, the Nimitz Freeway in Oakland, Calif., became a giant parking lot when a truck-trailer overturned, blocking traffic for 90 minutes.

Left, Michael and Sheree Ackerman spend a sad, tense moment in their daughter Melissa's room before going on the air to plead for the 7-year-old's return. The girl's body was found near the Ackerman home several days later.

Below, 13-year-old Bobby Smith is reunited with his mother and two sisters in Long Beach, Calif. He was missing for two years and was found in Providence, R.I. A 55-year-old drifter was subsequently convicted of kidnapping the boy.

AMANDA ALCOCK, CHICAGO SUN-TIMES

MICHAEL RONDOU, LONG BEACH (CALIF.) PRESS-TELEGRAM

Right, front entrance to the Florida State Prison.

Below, prisoner Raulerson passes time in his cell.

THIRD PLACE NEWSPAPER NEWS PICTURE STORY, BILL WAX, THE GAINESVILLE (FLA.) SUN (ALL PHOTOS PAGES 112-115)

The execution

After a decade of life behind bars on Florida's death row, James Raulerson was executed in the electric chair Jan. 20 for killing a policeman.

Photographer Bill Wax spent more than a year covering Raulerson's story. It was an attempt, he says, "to show the steps taken in executing an inmate, as well as to show the people involved."

Raulerson stares out of his cell. Since cameras have not been allowed on Florida's death row since the early 1970s, pictures of the condemned man were made with a concealed camera.

Above, prison Chaplain Ron Walker talks about Christ and the life hereafter with Raulerson.

Right, a view of "Old Sparky," the instrument of execution, with phone hookups to the prison superintendent and the governor. The view is through the glass as seen by witnesses.

The execution

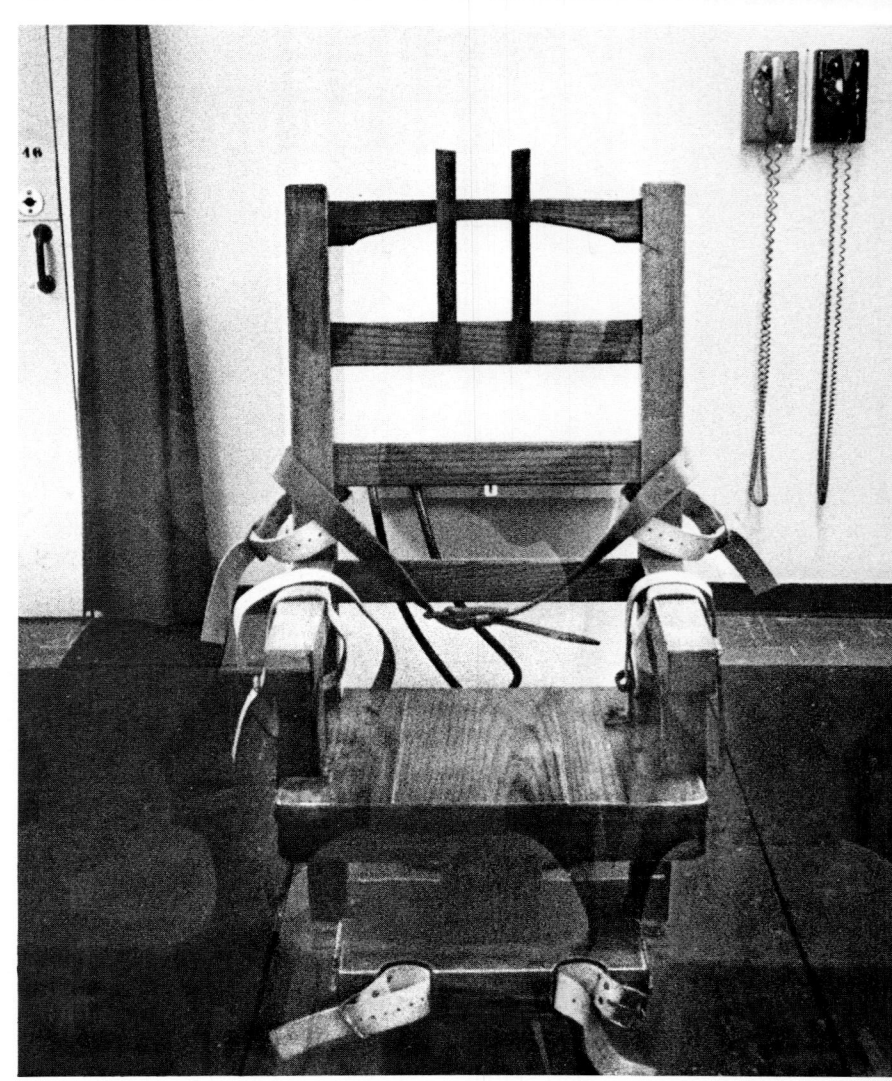

Above, a member of the Jacksonville sheriff's department cheers as the hearse containing Raulerson's body passes.

Left, three opponents of capital punishment hold an early morning vigil outside the prison to mourn Raulerson's death.

Right, Alice Brandenburg made medical history in Kentucky in August 1984 as the state's first heart transplant patient. Here she shows her despondency after being re-admitted to the hospital for more surgery. She died in July 1985.

JAY B. MATHER, THE COURIER-JOURNAL AND LOUISVILLE (KY.) TIMES

STEVE MELLON, THE HERALD (JASPER, IND.)

Above, Bill Schroeder, the world's longest living artificial heart recipient, was greeted by about 150 friends and relatives on his first trip home to Jasper, Ind., 253 days after his heart implant operation.

Above, easily 1985's most famous sea lion: Herschel, who upset biologists and anglers by feeding on coho salmon and steelhead trout making their way through Puget Sound to spawn. Herschel eventually was induced to leave.

GRANT M. HALLER, SEATTLE POST-INTELLIGENCER

Above, Gay Mullins of Seattle gets victory shower after Coca-Cola officials announced they'd resume bottling "old" Coke. As president of Old Cola Drinkers of America, Mullins led fight to keep the time-honored drink on the market.

HARLEY SOLTES, THE SEATTLE TIMES

Right, Pandit Kaleem Bai cries as she tells of her medical problems in the Hamidia Hospital outpatient clinic in Bhopal, India. She is one of the 10,000-plus survivors of the Bhopal Union Carbide gas tragedy — still seeking aid 10 months after the gas leak that killed hundreds.

PAULA BRONSTEIN, THE HARTFORD (CONN.) COURANT

These photographs are from a series produced in Nicaragua. Reported photographer John Gaps: "Intentional or not, war seems to hit hardest those who are too young and weak to defend themselves ... some are caught in the crossfire, many more are orphaned by the fighting ..."

JOHN GAPS III, THE KANSAS CITY (MO.) TIMES, BOTH PHOTOGRAPHS

Beirut bombings

Terrorism dominated the news out of the Middle East, which, reported the Associated Press, "continued to seethe in hatred." In mid-August, violence rocked Lebanon as a car bomb in Christian east Beirut killed 50 persons. Two days later, a bomb in Muslim west Beirut killed 29, wounded 82.

Right, a Christian Lebanese woman is helped away from the scene of a car bomb explosion in the east Beirut suburb of Saad El-Boushrieh.

ARISTOTLE SARICOSTAS, ASSOCIATED PRESS
HERVE MERLIAC, ASSOCIATED PRESS

Above, a Moslem gunner rests his hand on a 75mm rocket launcher as he peers toward Christian east Beirut.

Left, a family takes shelter under a bridge in west Beirut during a heavy artillery barrage.

LAMAA, AGENCE FRANCE-PRESSE
JAMAL SAIIDI, ASSOCIATED PRESS

Above, a Moslem father carries his son toward help after a car bomb blast in west Beirut

TOMMY PRICE, THE VIRGINIAN-PILOT/LEDGER-STAR (NORFOLK, VA.)
BARRY THUMMA, ASSOCIATED PRESS

Above, a student from Virginia's Liberty University tries to make friends with boys of the Beja tribe in the Sudan. The American was part of a team of students sent to aid the Sudanese.

Right, a frail Eritrean child sits in a medical tent at Wad Sherife refugee camp in the Sudan near the Ethiopian border. At one point the camp ran out of food for four days. The camp housed about 60,000 refugees.

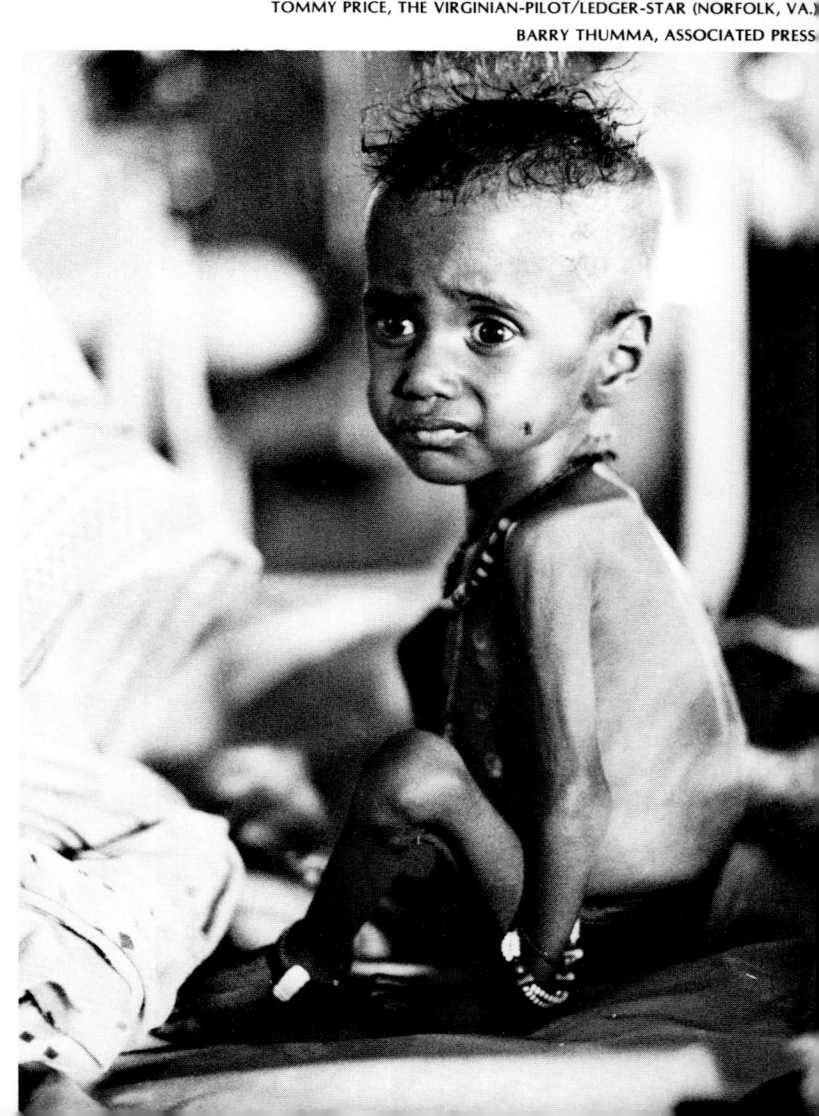

RALPH FITZGERALD, FREELANCE (NORFOLK, VA.)

RICK RICKMAN, ORANGE COUNTY REGISTER (SANTA ANA, CALIF.)

Above, Patty Frustaci became the mother of septuplets, but only three survived. Daughter Patricia was the first of the survivors to be released from Childrens Hospital in Orange County, Calif. When mother and daughter left the hospital, says Photographer Rick Rickman, "the pack closed in."

Left, convicted spy Arthur J. Walker leaves Norfolk, Va., Federal Courthouse after being convicted of seven counts of espionage. He is the brother of John Walker, the so-called master spy, who is also believed to have recruited his son and a Navy friend.

123

RICHARD LIPSKI, THE WASHINGTON POST

First Lady Nancy Reagan tries her hand (and feet) at flamenco dancing with a young Spanish dancer during her visit with the President to Madrid, Spain, in May.

Actor Yul Brynner takes a curtain call after his 4,625th and final appearance as the lead in "The King and I." He died of cancer at 65.

RICHARD LEE, NEW YORK NEWSDAY

Losing Max

Max Greenberg is 69 years old. He has forgotten his life.

Since the first symptoms of Alzheimer's disease appeared eight years ago, he has lost the ability to play dominoes, carry on a simple conversation, or find his way around his Bucks County (Pa.) apartment.

For Max, nothing exists but here and now. The one person he recognizes consistently is "Mommy," which is what he now calls his wife of 35 years.

When his wife, Bert, is away at work, or out shopping, Max is left at home with a sitter.

Bert loves Max fiercely. She fights to keep him at home with her as long as possible, and to preserve what's left of his mind.

Still, if Max's case follows the norm, the day will come when Bert can no longer care for him at home.

That is something she cannot think about.

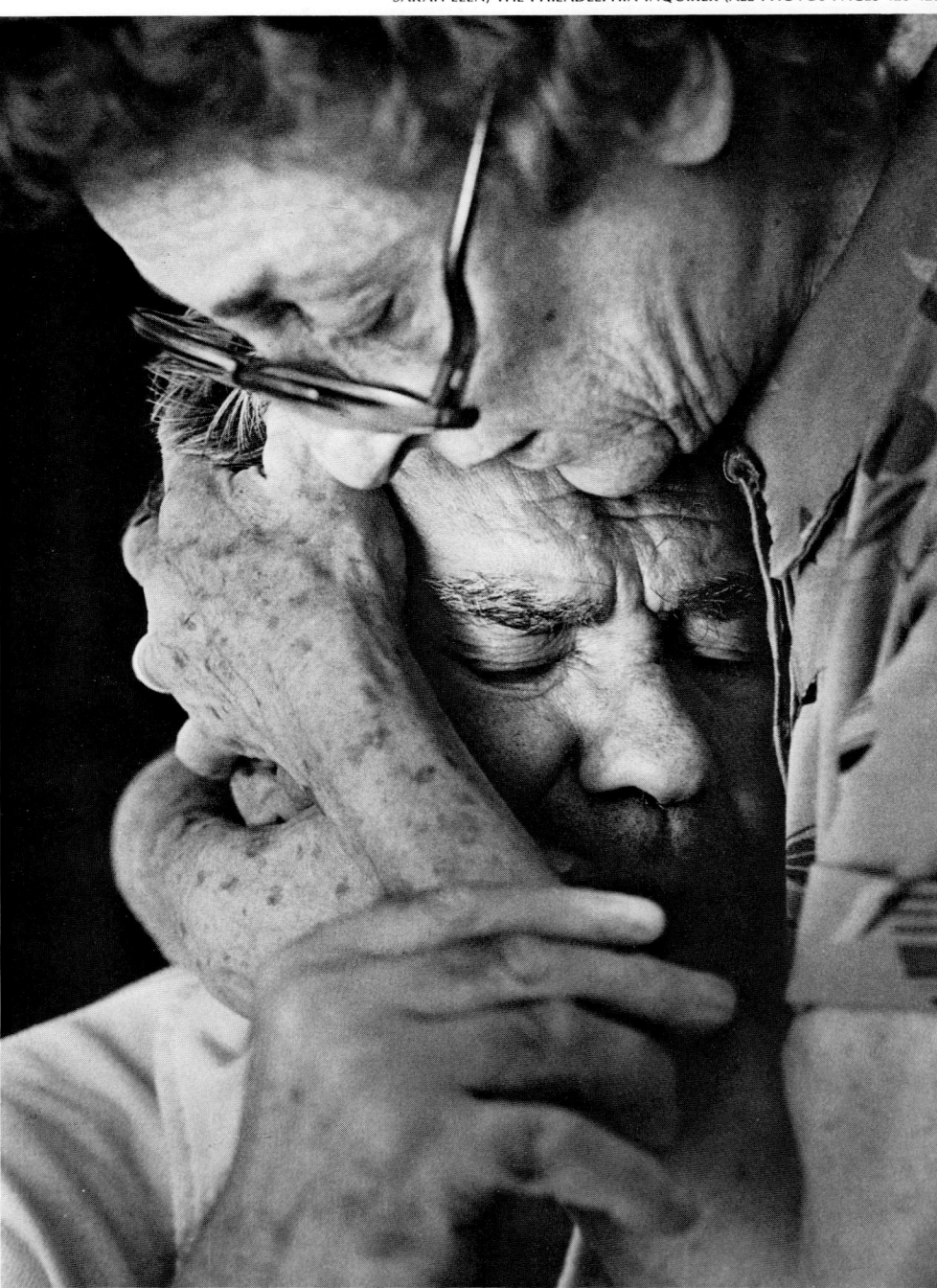

SARAH LEEN, THE PHILADELPHIA INQUIRER (ALL PHOTOS PAGES 126-129

"Max?"
"Yes."
"What's my name?"
"Mommy."
"Nope."
"Bert."
"Bert what?"
"Greenberg."
"And I am your? What am I to you?"
"You're my, you're my wife."
"That's right. And your name is?"
"Max."
"The whole name."
"Max Greenberg."
"Uh huh, very good, And you are my?"
(He sings) "Sunshine, my only sunshine, you make me happy when skies are grey. You'll never know, dear, how much I love you. Please don't take my sunshine away."

"Is this your room?"
"I suppose it was at one time, but not now, it's nothing now. I don't know what it is now, it's nothing but some clothes and stuff. I don't know whose things they are."

"I used to work him with a calendar every night, take about 15, 20 minutes to do the days of the week. Then it got too stressful for him, so the hell with that, can't do that to him. So that's why you see him swishing around with paint, with the crayons — to relieve that stress. I used to play dominoes with him — he used to be very good in dominoes — and when I found it was too stressful, it was upsetting him, I put the darn things away."

Losing Max —

"I'm in trouble. I think I'm crazy. I don't know what to do. I'm sick, I can't take care of myself, there's a pain inside my head. Mommy, Mommy."
"What, Max, what is it?"
"I don't know, Mommy, Mommy."
"What is it, Max? Tell me what it is."
"I want to go home. You take good care of me, Mommy. You're my Mommy. I feel sick, I feel like I have been hit in the head. Don't worry about me, I'll just go, I'll just die somewhere."

When there is no one to sit at home with Max, Bert takes him along on shopping trips. These outings can be especially stressful for Max, because of the unfamiliar surroundings. Here Bert gives him a playful chuck under the chin for being unusually cooperative at the grocery store.

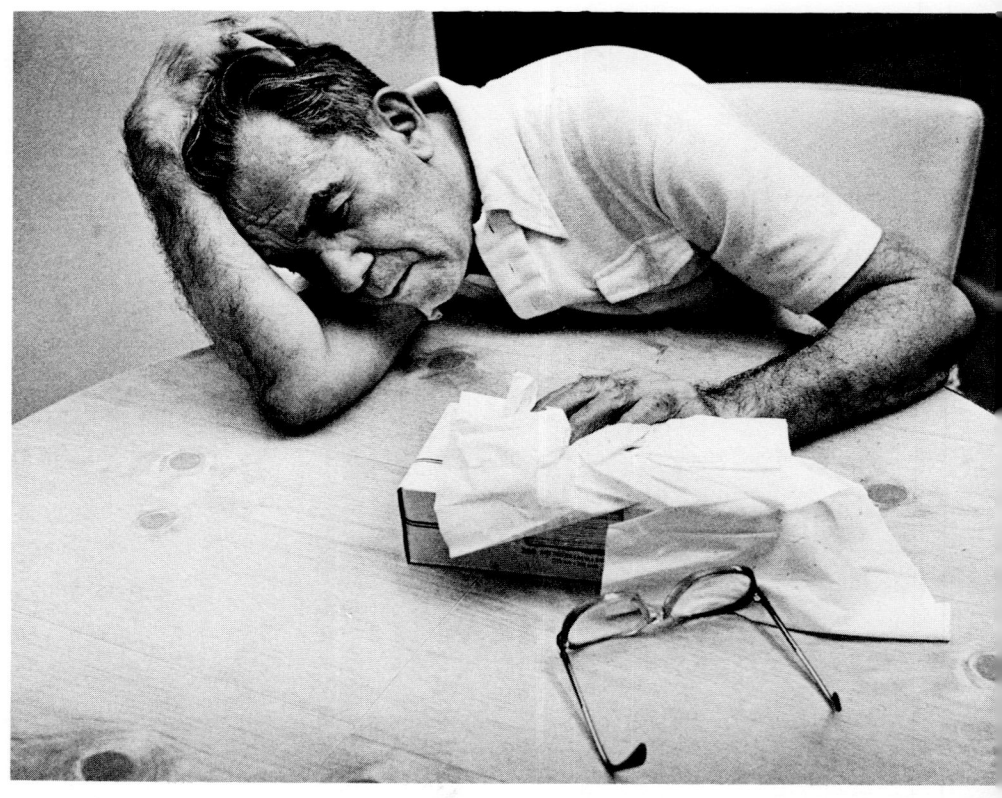

Max won't take a nap without his wife nearby. If she leaves the room, he gets up and follows. So Bert sits patiently until he falls asleep, then tries to sneak out of the room to do her work around the house.

"He keeps thinking I'm going to walk out. I don't know why. You never know what life has in store for you. You might as well get it as you can. Isn't it frightening to see a man like this?"

Charlie's ordeal

Charlie Willette was only three when fire destroyed his family's rural Minnesota home. He was burned so badly doctors said he was, statistically, 100 percent sure to die.

But Charlie didn't die. Instead, he spent six months at St. Luke's Hospital in Fargo, N.D., and then began daily, 90-mile round trips to the hospital for therapy.

Charlie wears a body suit and a mask to control scarring and tissue growth.

The youngster will receive daily therapy for a year, probably two. Says his doctor, "Any plastic surgery will have to come later."

Deb Willette, Charlie's mother, also was burned in the fire. Now she says: "Every day I ask myself, 'Why me?' More often, I ask, 'Why Charlie?'"

Right, Charlie and his younger brother Jeff, who also suffered third-degree burns, ride tricycles outside the family's trailer house. Below, Charlie winces as a doctor adjusts his mask and splint. The splint keeps his arm extended at a 90-degree angle and helps prevent potential webbing under his arm.

THIRD PLACE NEWSPAPER FEATURE PICTURE STORY, TOM SWEENEY, MINNEAPLIS (MINN.) STAR-TRIBUNE (BOTH PAGES)

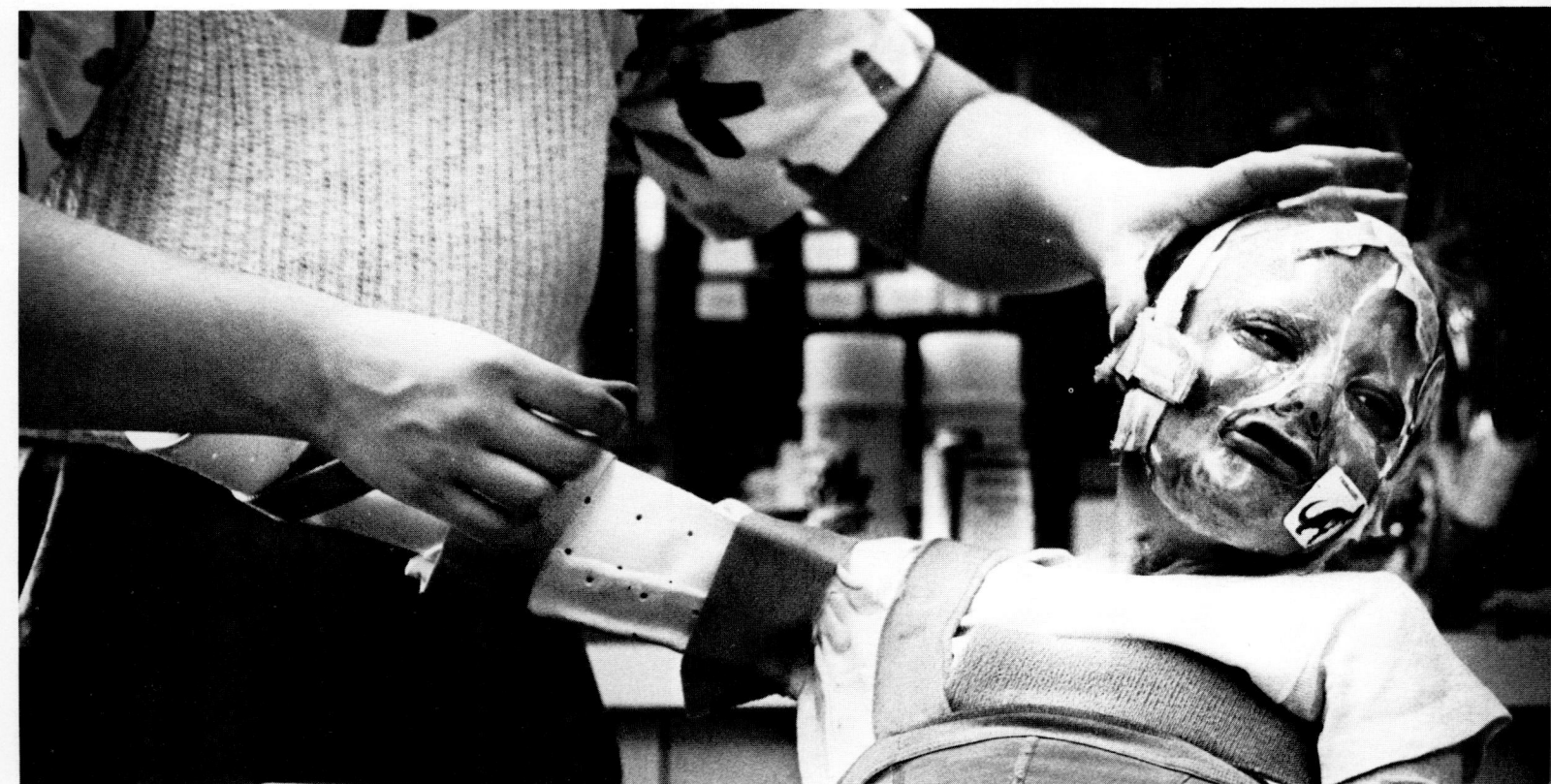

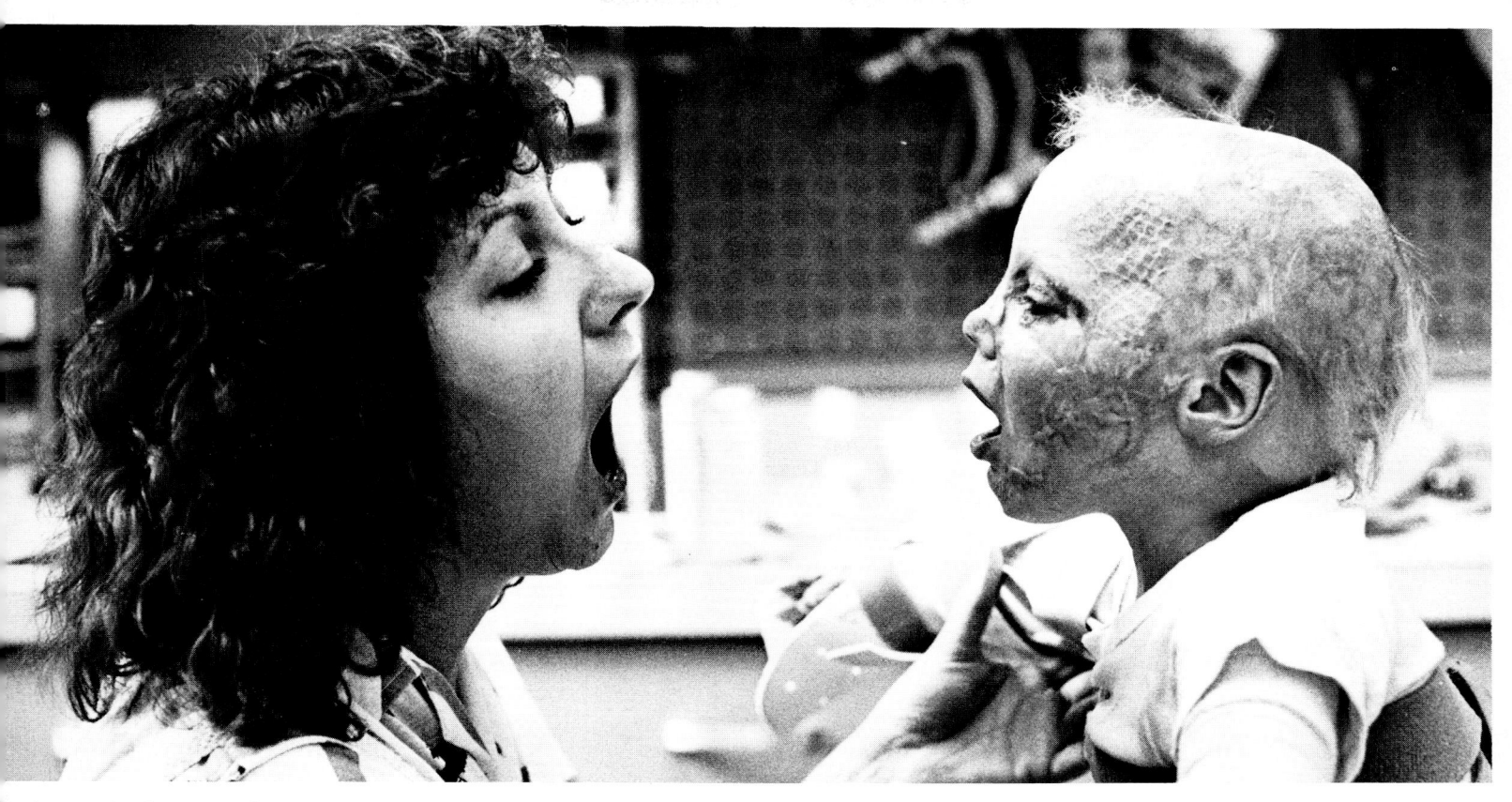

Below, Charlie threads a wooden bead during a physical therapy session.

Above, occupational therapist Karen Sevigny helps with mouth-stretching exercises.

Below, with a warm hug, Sevigny sends Charlie off to another therapist at the end of their daily session.

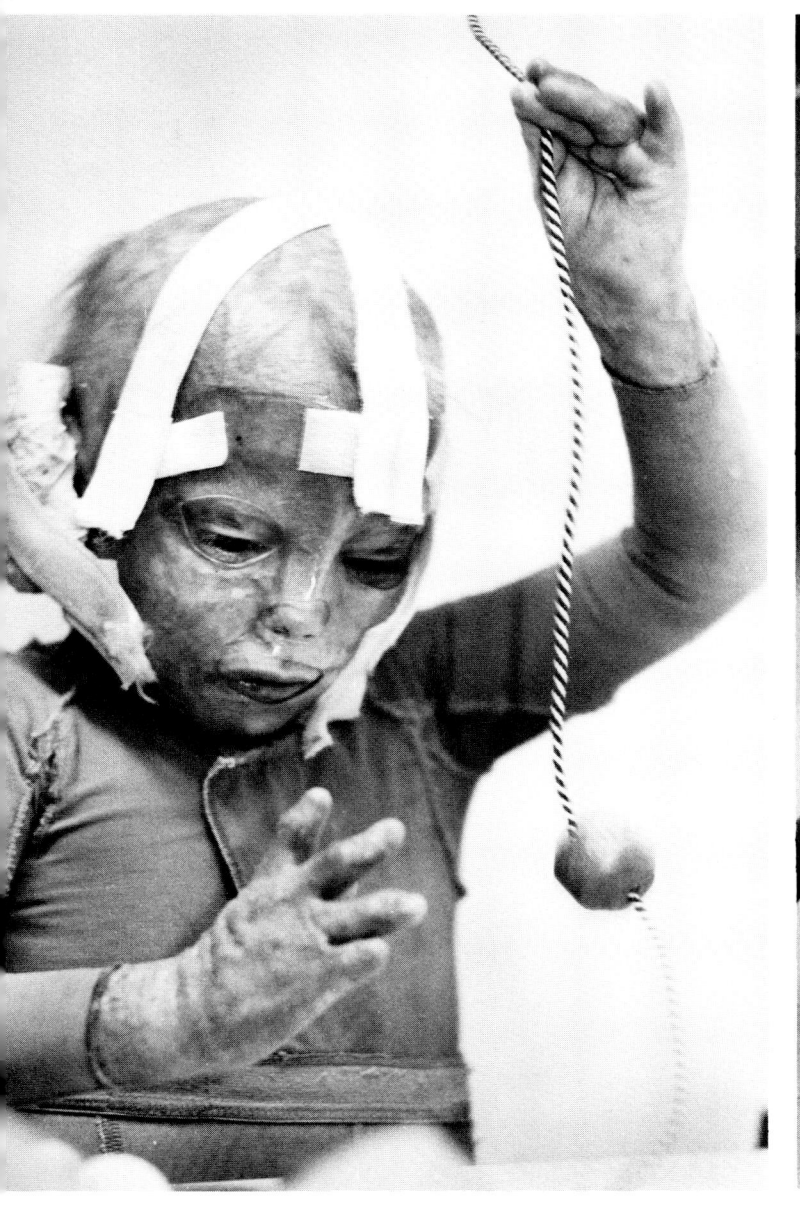

No '30' for J.S.

He's called the oldest working journalist in the country: 97-year-old J.S. Moran, editor emeritus of the Springfield, Ky., Sun, who comes to the office every morning, and shows no inclination to quit.

Moran bought the Sun in 1916 and sold it to Landmark Communications 56 years later. These days, he writes a column, and delivers the paper to downtown merchants.

Moran has lived through three eras of newspaper technology change and admits journalism "is the only thing I ever wanted to do."

How does he regard his readers? "My philosophy when we disagree is not to be disagreeable," he says. "They're entitled to their opinion, but it doesn't change mine a bit."

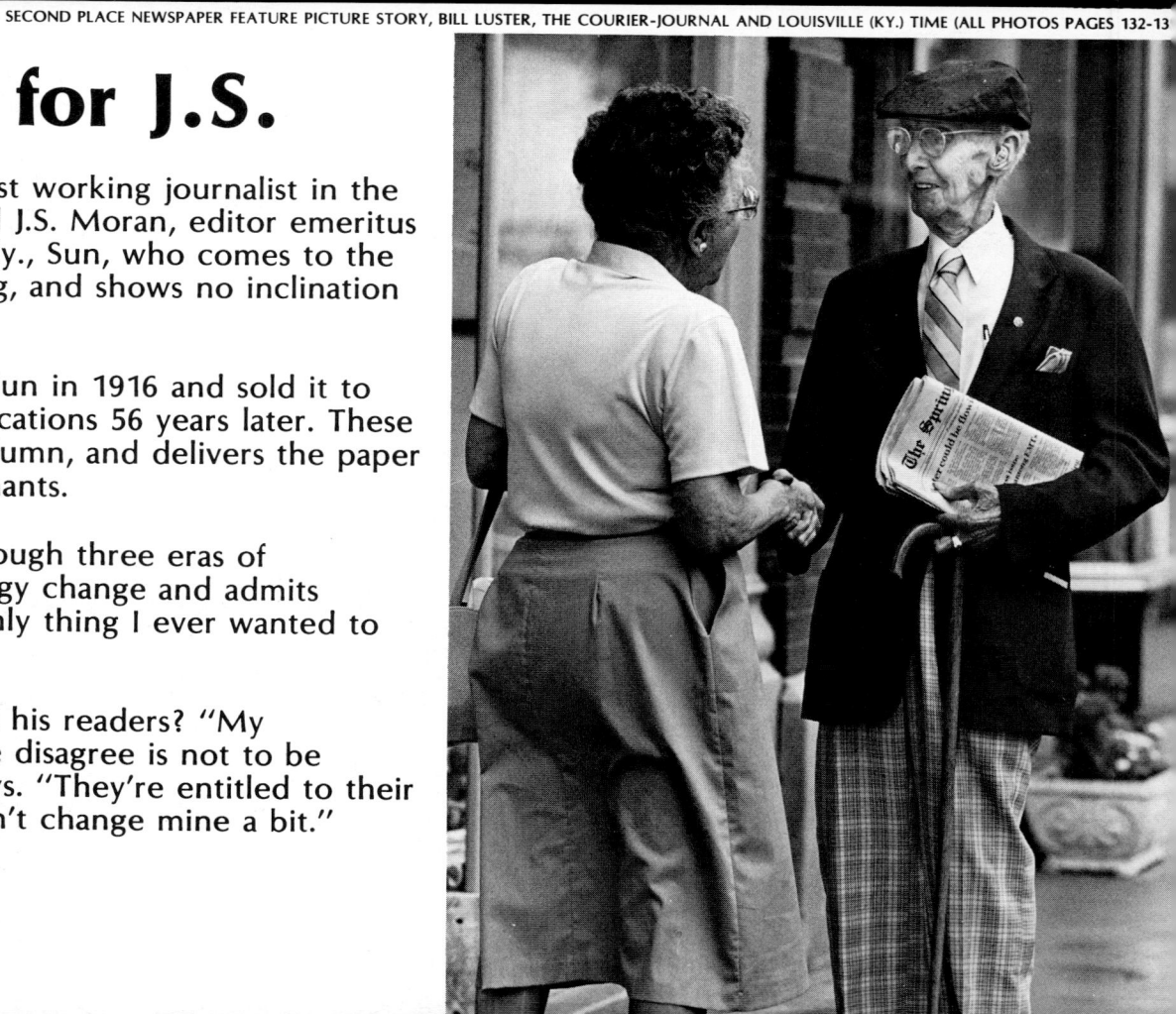

Moran leafs through his notes, then focuses his attention on the old Underwood he's used since Dwight Eisenhower was president.

Oldest journalis

When he covered an appearance of President Jimmy Carter in Bardstown, Ky., Moran was the oldest journalist ever accredited by the White House.

Top, Moran's office is right behind the office of young editor John Bramel. Bottom, Moran leaves the office shortly after lunch, as usual.

Right, mail carrier Minette Sheller had residents on her route in Reseda, Calif., wondering just what she was going to deliver today.

Below, making her day, Ruie LeMaster, 81, takes careful aim with a squirt gun in a pistol competition. It was all part of a Junior-Senior Olympics at a Henderson, Ky., nursing home.

AL SEIB, LOS ANGELES TIMES

FIRST PLACE NEWSPAPER FEATURE, BOB GWALTNEY, THE EVANSVILLE (IND.) PRESS

THIRD PLACE NEWSPAPER HUMOR, ARTHUR POLLOCK, THE BOSTON HERALD

Above, all that form and grace is great, but one student at the Lexington School of Ballet in Boston had her fill.

Below, kindergarten graduate Kathryn Cowles reacts to the commencement address during ceremonies at the Murray Language Academy in Chicago's Hyde Park.

SECOND PLACE NEWSPAPER FEATURE, RICH HEIN, THE CHICAGO SUN-TIMES

Above, the Behm family of Merztown, Pa., enjoys ice cream at a roadside stand on a hot August evening.

DON FISHER, THE MORNING CALL (ALLENTOWN, PA.)

Below, young men from a New Jersey rehabilitation center for juveniles convicted of serious crimes are helping restore some of the old buildings in the historic community of Whitesbog Village.

MICHAEL A. BAYTOFF, ATLANTIC CITY (N.J.) PRESS

JUDY GRIESDIECK, SAN JOSE (CALIF.) MERCURY NEWS

Above, after spending the earlier part of their lives as strangers in a foreign land, living in the shadows of their husbands, this group of elderly Japanese imigrant women share a home in California.

Below, it took this crew eight weeks to dismantle a 1,250-ton hydraulic bending press after the closing of the Foster Wheeler Energy Corp. plant in Mountaintop, Pa.

ARNOLD GOLD, THE TIMES LEADER (WILKES-BARRE, PA.)

139

JEFF GREENE, THE JOURNAL (LORAIN, OHIO)

Above, a worker in Lorain, Ohio, cleans snow from a fire escape at the Moose Lodge.

Below, Diane Petersen, umbrella well in hand, heads for work in Ogden, Utah.

STEVE JONES, OGDEN (UTAH) STANDARD EXAMINER

AL FUCHS, THE ORANGE COUNTY REGISTER (SANTA ANA, CALIF.)

Above, guest at Disneyland Hotel in Anaheim, Calif., checks the territory.

MICHAEL GALLACHER, THE MISSOULIAN (MISSOULA, MONT.)

Above, in Missoula, Mont., an Exxon employee climbs a 630,000-gallon storage tank to retrieve a sample of the gasoline within.

STEVEN R. NICKERSON, THE LEXINGTON (KY.) HERALD-LEADER

Above, painter goes the extra mile, doing his part to restore Victorian Square, a major downtown renewal project in Lexington, Ky.

CHUCK BERMAN, CHICAGO TRIBUNE

DAN SIEFERT, THE KANSAS CITY (MO.) STAR

GARY FONG, SAN FRANCISCO CHRONICLE

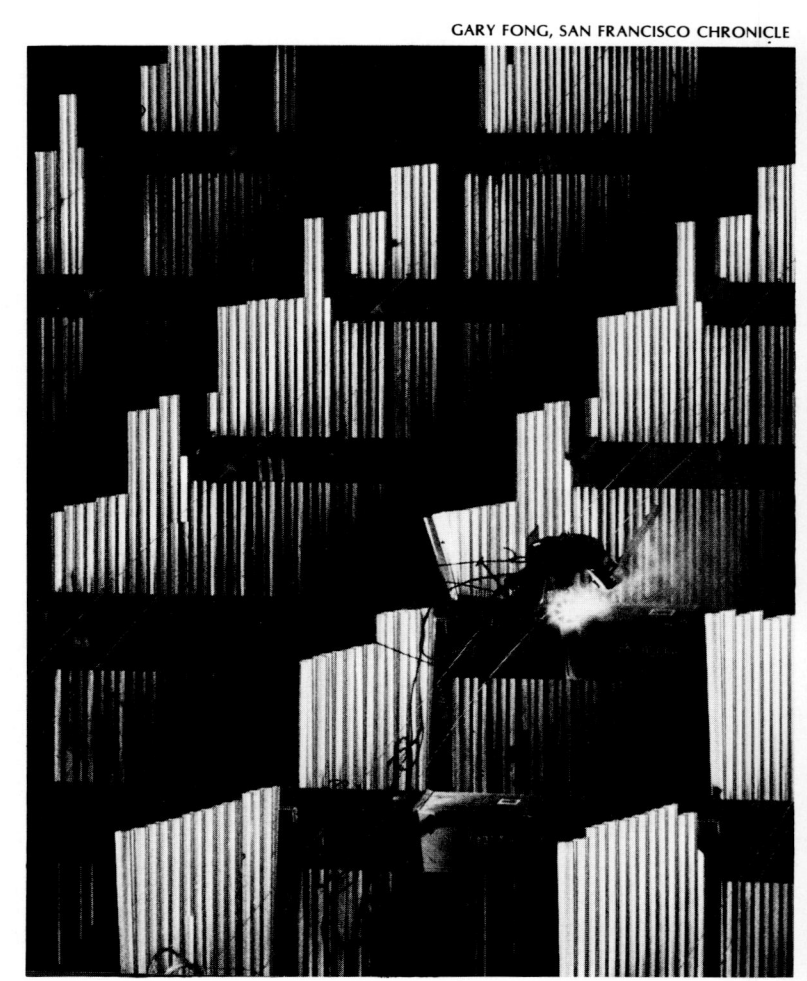

Upper left, winter in Chicago can be a study in patterns, textures - and snow shovels.

Upper right, Kansas City carpenter checks the alignment of steel reinforcing bars on a highway construction job.

Right, ironworker is center of attention in picture from an 18-month assignment to photograph the birth of a 26-story San Francisco skyscraper.

HENRY DiROCCO, LOS ANGELES TIMES

Above, 2-year-old Nathan Walton uses a wooden playground structure as cover in a game of hide and seek with his mother in Anaheim, Calif.

Below, mailman Richard Bixler works his way down a rack of mailboxes at a trailer park in East Windsor, Conn.

MIKE ADASKAVEG, JOURNAL INQUIRER, MANCHESTER, CONN.

RAYMOND GEHMAN, THE VIRGINIAN-PILOT LEDGER-STAR, (NORFOLK, VA.)
THIRD PLACE NEWSPAPER EDITORIAL ILLUSTRATION, JIM MAYFIELD, SPRINGFIELD (MO.) NEWSPAPERS, INC.

Above, karate enthusiasts brave the brisk, 45-degree waters of the Atlantic Ocean during a workout designed to improve strength and discipline.

Right, life-sized 6-month-old Katie O'Dell gets a close-up view of larger-than-life painting, "Gorilla," at Springfield, Mo., Art Museum.

SECOND PLACE NEWSPAPER PICTORIAL, CHRIS RUSSELL, THE NEWS-HERALD (WILLOUGHBY, OHIO)

Above, Bill and Pat Hudec of Painesville, Ohio, enjoy a drive-in movie — and their 1957 Ford convertible.

SECOND PLACE NEWSPAPER EDITORIAL ILLUSTRATION, GARY FANDEL, THE DES MOINES (IOWA) REGISTER

Above, back pain problems get graphic in Des Moines.

Left, apple's-eye view of a childhood tradition makes Halloween art.

FIRST PLACE NEWSPAPER EDITORIAL ILLUSTRATION, JEFF ALEXANDER, THE ALBUQUERQUE (N.M.) JOURNAL

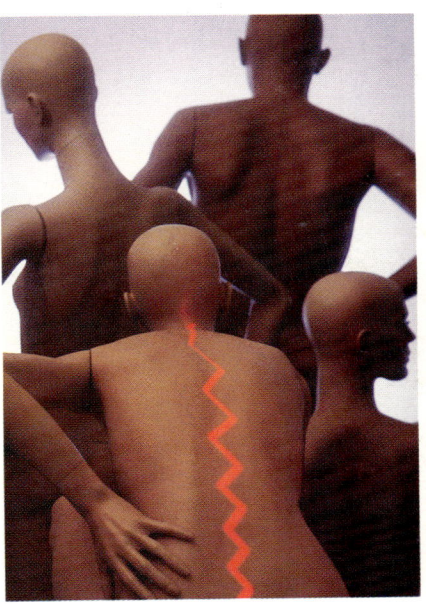

145

GRANT M. HALLER, SEATTLE POST-INTELLIGENCER

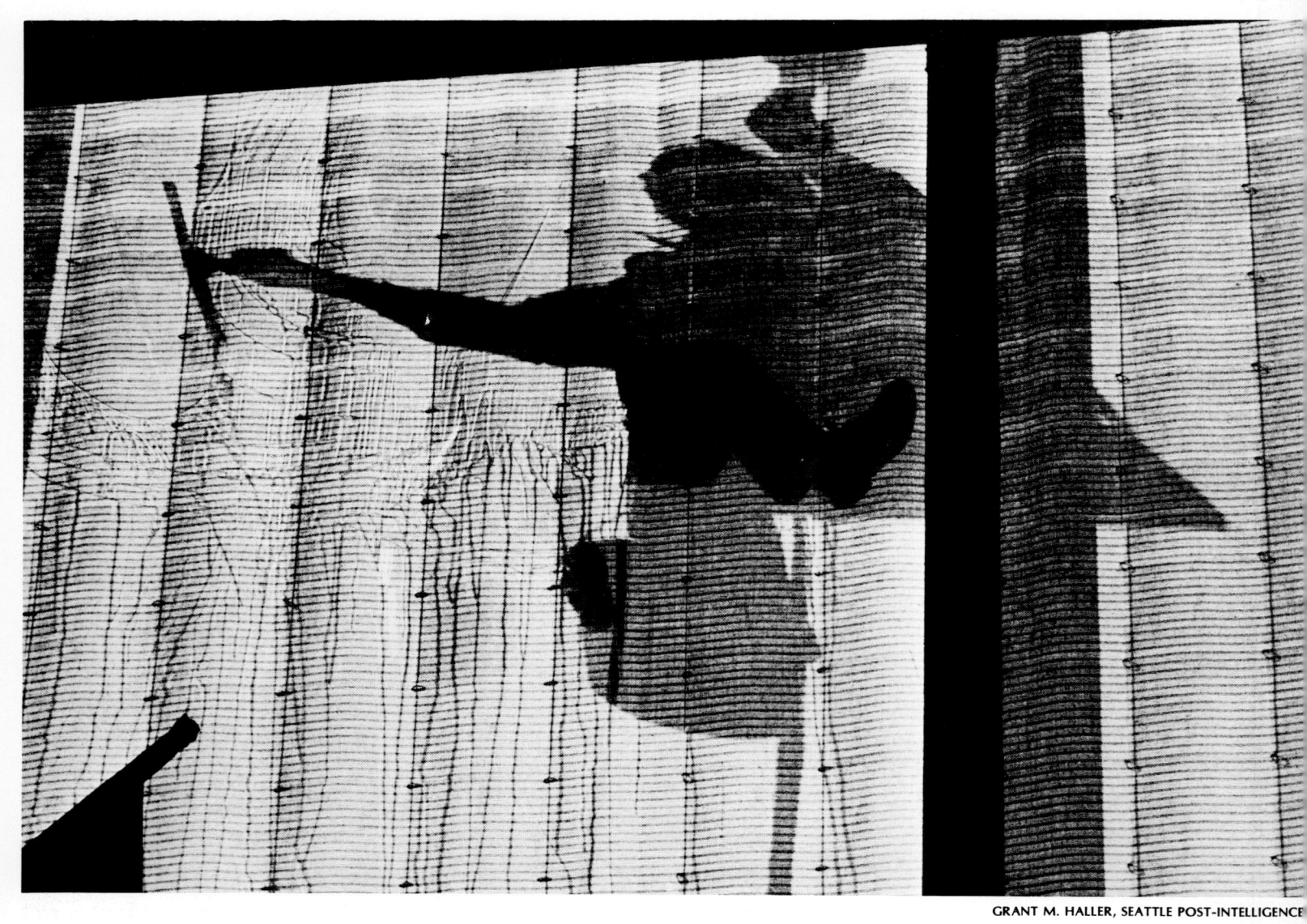

Silhouette and shadow of a window washer play on a window and blinds at Edgewater Inn, Seattle, Wash.

DAVID C. TILLERY, SAN ANGELO (TEXAS) STANDARD-TIMES

Above, despite all the benefits of a computerized age, an old house still comes down one board at a time. This one was in San Angelo, Texas.

Below, Evelyn Higgins performs her own brand of levitation while cleaning window blinds.

KEVIN G. GEIL, THE ROUND ROCK (TEXAS) LEADER

SECOND PLACE NEWSPAPER FOOD ILLUSTRATION, MICHAEL P. FRANKLIN, SAN DIEGO (CALIF.) UNION/TRIBUNE

THIRD PLACE NEWSPAPER FOOD ILLUSTRATION, SCOTT ROBINSON, THE PROVIDENCE (R.I.) JOURNAL

Above, Photographer Michael Franklin isn't saying how he got the champagne to jump out of the glass.

Below, Photographer Alan Berner says Hood Canal shrimp are best photographed as cooked: simply, with lemon.

Above, Photographer Scott Robinson says the secret of his fruit torte picture is (a) black spray paint, (b) a grid screen.

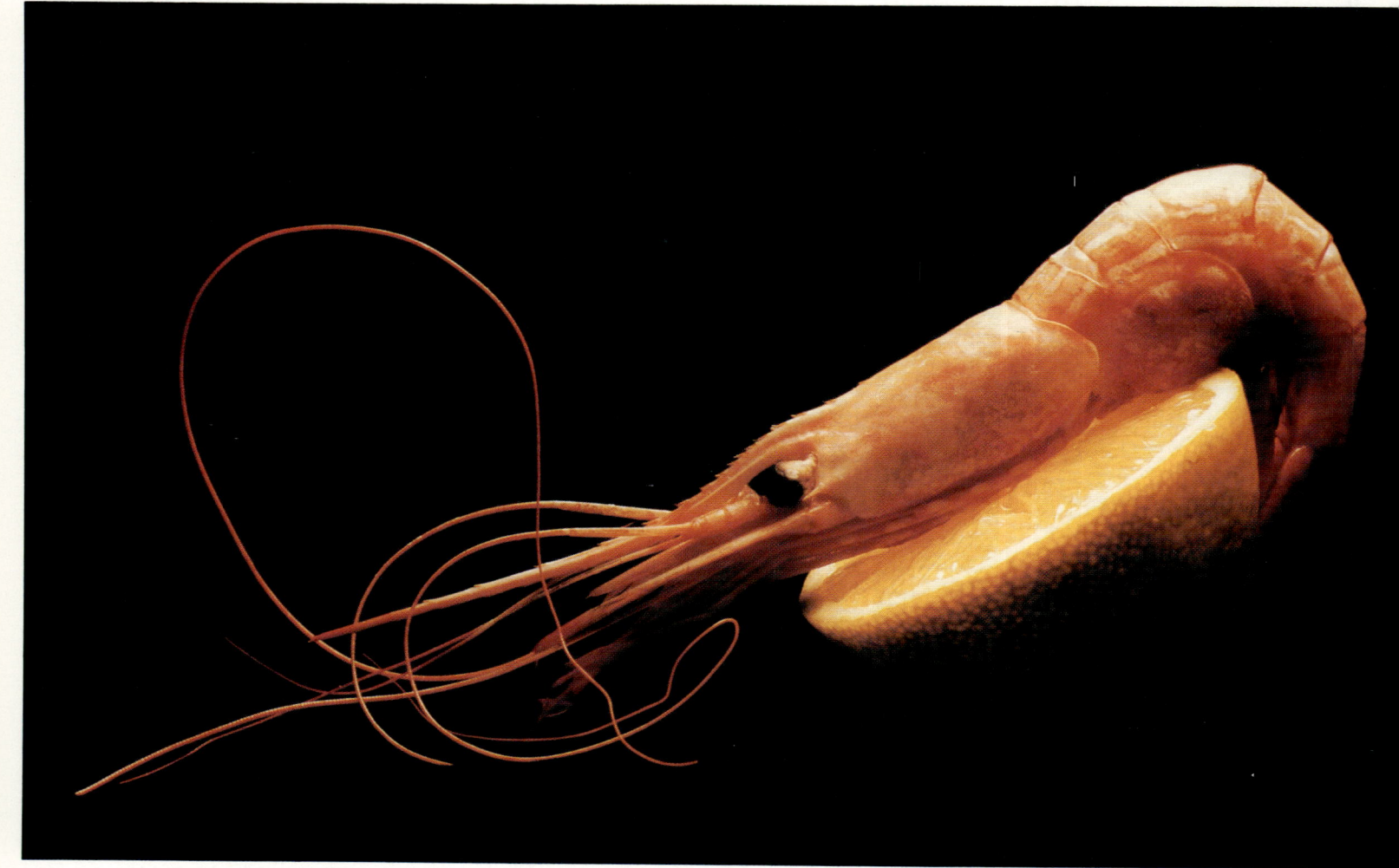

FIRST PLACE NEWSPAPER FOOD ILLUSTRATION, ALAN BERNER, THE SEATTLE TIMES

SECOND PLACE NEWSPAPER FASHION ILLUSTRATION, MURRAY SILL, THE MIAMI HERALD

bove, Problem: show how to dress or the hot south Florida climate. olution: hot spots.

Below, problem: illustrate the drama and verve of red shoes. Solution: black and white photography — almost.

Below, problem: illustrate the texture of autumn shoe fashions. Solution: black and white photography — almost.

FIRST PLACE NEWSPAPER FASHION ILLUSTRATION, CRAIG TRUMBO, THE FLORIDA TIMES-UNION (JACKSONVILLE)

THIRD PLACE NEWSPAPER FASHION ILLUSTRATION, ERWIN GEBHARD, THE MILWAUKEE JOURNAL

SUSAN STEINKAMP, SYRACUSE (N.Y.) NEWSPAPER

Above, a ewe with its head in a can got much attention but no help from a trio of ponies. The owner of the animals came quickly to the rescue on a farm near Syracuse, N.Y.

Below, Pa, a 5,000-pound rhinoceros, went head to head with a mechanical monster when Pa and the entire animal population of Marine World in Redwood City, Calif., were moved to new digs in Vallejo.

JOE MELENA, TIMES TRIBUNE (PALO ALTO, CALIF.)

PAUL O'NEILL, THE MESA (ARIZ.) TRIBUNE

Above, get curious about a garbage can and now look. The temptation, of course, is to call it canned beef. (A passer-by went into the steer's pasture near Mesa, Ariz., and did the honors.)

VALERIE HODGSON, FREELANCE (BROOKLYN, N.Y.)

Meet Nuka the walrus, who turned the tables by staring back at visitors to the New York Aquarium in Coney Island.

JEFF SHAW, DALLAS TIMES HERALD

Only in Texas, perhaps, but this resident of Duncanville brings her horse to the car wash for a hosing-down every week.

FIRST PLACE MAGAZINE SPORTS, MICKEY PFLEGER, FREELANCE FOR TIME

THIRD PLACE MAGAZINE SPORTS, PETER MENZEL, FREELANCE (NAPA, CALIF.)

Above, St. Louis Cardinal shortstop Ozzie Smith does his pre-game routine before game five of the 1985 World Series.

Below, framed by hoop and cornfields, three Indiana youngsters go for ball.

Above, air instructors perform a hot dog maneuver: a three-man ring in a padded flight chamber.

SECOND PLACE MAGAZINE SPORTS, JOE McNALLY, FREELANCE (NEW YORK CITY)

152

FIRST PLACE MAGAZINE SCIENCE/NATURAL HISTORY, PETER MENZEL, FREELANCE (NAPA, CALIF.)

Photographer Peter Menzel made a double exposure to record both moon and dawn in this photograph of a windfarm that he calls "Tehachapi windmills."

Coming down from a tree with the remains of a kill, this leopard is heading for the brush.

SECOND PLACE (ABOVE), THIRD PLACE (BELOW) MAGAZINE SCIENCE/NATURAL HISTORY, STEPHEN J. KRASEMANN, NATIONAL GEOGRAPHIC

In Ngorongoro Crater, Tanzania, a flock of crowned cranes takes flight.

THIRD PLACE NEWSPAPER PICTORIAL, BRANT WARD, SAN FRANCISCO CHRONICLE

Oops ... above, Patch, an English pointer, is outwitted by a quail during his first training session of the season at a club near Sacramento, Calif.

Below, Chuck Harrison was really hoping for a Christmas goose as he hunted in California's Central Valley. His yellow Lab, Annie, couldn't have cared less.

FIRST PLACE NEWSPAPER HUMOR, ERIC LUSE, SAN FRANCISCO CHRONICLE

bill alkofer, THE REGISTER (SANTA ANA, CALIF.)

Above, talk about following the leader; apparently there isn't a sign reader in this whole flock.

Slap a ram on the rump (below) and see what happens. This high-jumping Dorset (aka Sport) reacted to a well-aimed swat on the behind as it was being herded to a washing stall on the Iowa State Fairgrounds.

BOB NANDELL, THE DES MOINES (IOWA) REGISTER

155

FIRST PLACE MAGAZINE ILLUSTRATION, GARY CHAPMAN, THE COURIER-JOURNAL AND LOUISVILLE (KY.) TIMES

Assigned to illustrate a story on "off-the-wall-DJs," Photographer Gary Chapman and his art director worked 40 hours to build this set (and — after the photograph was made — another hour to tear it down).

SECOND PLACE MAGAZINE ILLUSTRATION, GILLES TAPIE, TIME
THIRD PLACE MAGAZINE ILLUSTRATION, BRIAN HAGIWARA FOR CONNOISSEUR

A model displays designer Issey Miyake's high-fashion coat.

Photographer Brian Hagiwara's assignment was to show the how and why of exotic fruits and vegetables.

157

CHRISTOPHER FITZGERALD, MIDDLESEX NEWS (FRAMINGHAM, MASS.)

JOE M. BARRERA JR., SAN ANTONIO (TEXAS) EXPRESS AND NEWS

Above, a house in Milford, Mass., was split in two so it could be more easily moved to a new location.

Below, movers took five days in April to move San Antonio's Hotel Fairmount six blocks. The brick structure is the heaviest building (3.2 million pounds) ever to be moved on wheeled dollies.

Above, a Victorian Florida cracker house is poised on the crest of a bridge while being towed from downtown Fort Pierce, Fla., to become part of a county museum.

JON KRAL, THE MIAMI HERALD

A decoy police officer arrests a mugger on a New York subway. Photographer Bruce Davidson rode with the decoys three weeks waiting for this moment.

FIRST PLACE MAGAZINE FEATURE, BRUCE DAVIDSON, NEW YORK MAGAZINE

A head by two feet: soaking in a health-giving hot spring pool near the Japan Sea in Fukuura. High iron content makes water brown.

SECOND PLACE MAGAZINE FEATURE, LYNN JOHNSON, A DAY IN THE LIFE OF JAPAN

At a party following honors ceremony at Washington, D.C.'s Kennedy Center, a hired entertainer exposes herself to unsuspecting guests.

RIGHT, THIRD PLACE MAGAZINE FEATURE, DIANA WALKER, TIME

FIRST PLACE MAGAZINE PORTRAIT/PERSONALITY, JON WARREN, WORLD CONCERN MAGAZINE

A Khmer Rouge refugee girl awaits treatment in a crowded hospital at a refugee camp on the Thai-Cambodia border.

THIRD PLACE MAGAZINE PICTURE STORY, STEPHEN SHAMES, ALICIA PATTERSON FOUNDATION

Among the nation's homeless: Mike Wallace of Ventura, Calif., shown with son Charlie, 6. The Wallaces and their five children live in a 6 by 13-foot trailer in McGrath State Park.

DON FISHER, THE MORNING CALL, ALLENTOWN, PA.

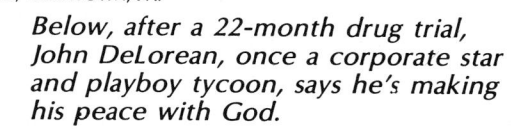

AL PODGORSKI, THE CHICAGO SUN-TIM[ES]

Above, Chrysler chief Lee A. Iacocca wrote a best-selling book and directed renovation of the Statue of Liberty.

Below, after a 22-month drug trial, John DeLorean, once a corporate star and playboy tycoon, says he's making his peace with God.

Above, Mother Teresa cradles Maria Halley in a public appearance in Chicago where she helped open a new shelter for her missionaries.

MICHELE McDONALD, THE VIRGINIAN-PILOT AND THE LEDGER-STAR (NORFOLK, V[A])

RAY STUBBLEBINE, ASSOCIATED PRESS

Watching undercover police question subway fare-cheaters, New York Mayor Ed Koch peers through a peephole. Some 640 persons were stopped, and 140 of them arrested.

NEWSPAPER PHOTOGRAPHER OF THE YEAR
STEVE RINGMAN, SAN FRANCISCO CHRONICLE

Above, Bruce Springsteen performs live in Oakland. Right, more than 2,000 women answered the casting call when ex-lead Van Halen singer David Lee Roth, embarking on a movie career, held auditions for his first film.

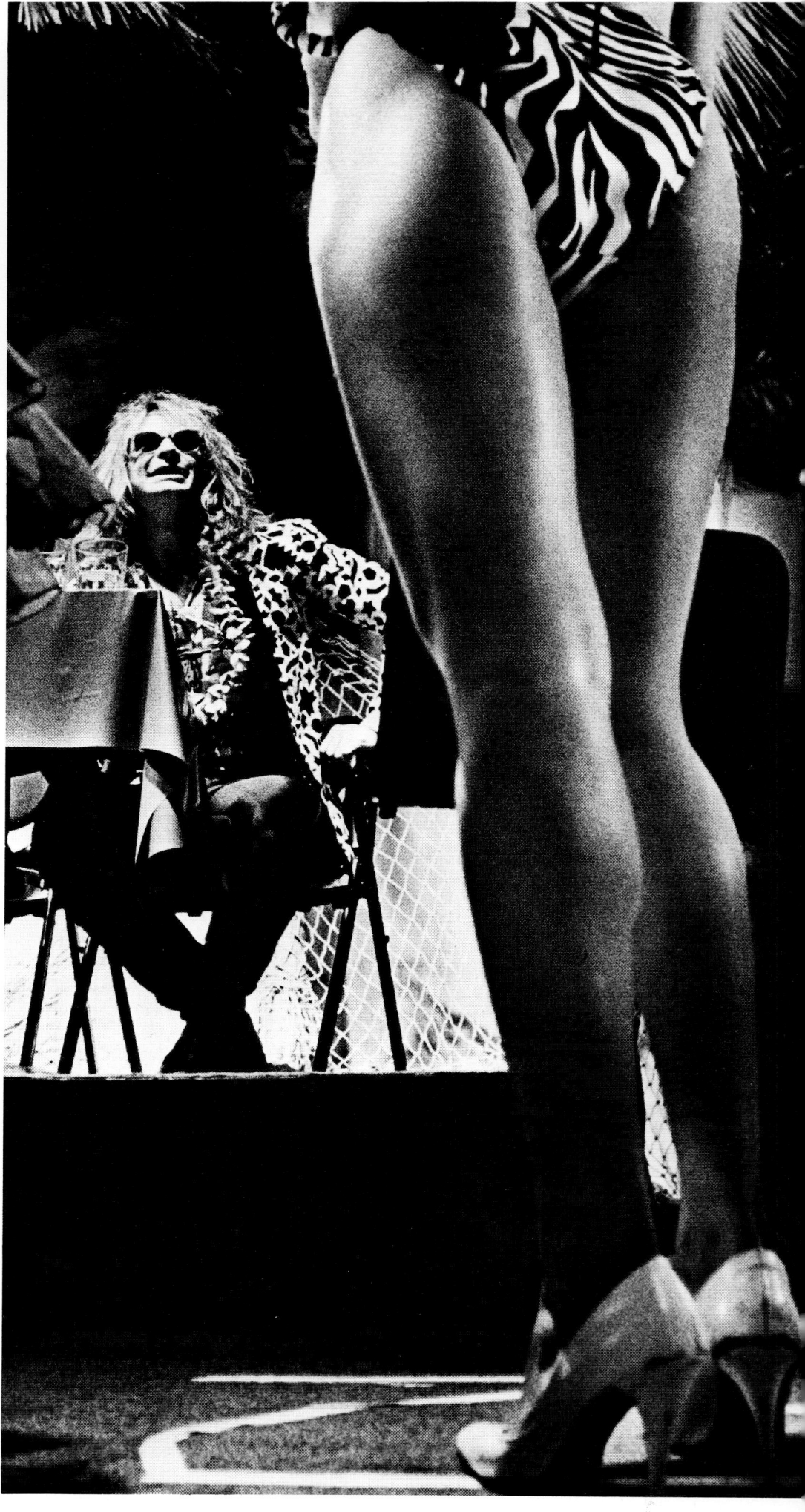

SECOND PLACE NEWSPAPER
PORTRAIT/PERSONALITY, TOM JAGOE,
LOS ANGELES DAILY NEWS

ANACLETO RAPPING, LOS ANGELES TIMES
ACEY HARPER, USA TODAY

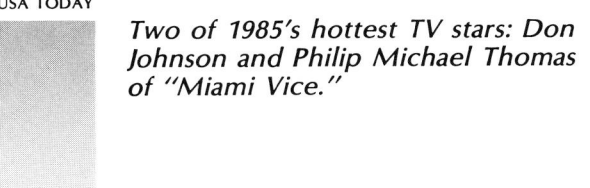

One of 1985's hottest rock stars: Phil Collins, on stage during his "No Jacket Required" tour.

Two of 1985's hottest TV stars: Don Johnson and Philip Michael Thomas of "Miami Vice."

Above, Grace Jones at a press conference for the opening of the James Bond film, "A View to a Kill." Below, actress Whoopi Goldberg, photographed during production of the film, "The Color Purple." Right, Muhammad Ali gets a facial in his home town of Louisville, Ky., during a Christmas visit to his mother.

FIRST PLACE NEWSPAPER PORTRAIT/PERSONALITY, CHRIS HARDY, SAN FRANCISCO EXAMINER

SCOTT GOLDSMITH, THE COURIER-JOURNAL AND LOUISVILLE (KY.) TIMES

MARK B. SLUDER, THE CHARLOTTE (N.C.) OBSERVER

NEWSPAPER PHOTOGRAPHER OF THE YEAR, STEVE RINGMAN, SAN FRANCISCO CHRONICLE

Above, Robert Cray is a musician from the Northwest whose blues music originates in the Deep South.

TOM CRUZE, THE CHICAGO SUN-TIMES

Above, everyone's an Irishman on St. Patrick's Day, including Ramon Cervantes, who's all ready for the Chicago Paddy's Day parade.

THIRD PLACE NEWSPAPER PHOTOGRAPHER OF THE YEAR, ERIC LUSE, SAN FRANCISCO CHRONICLE

Salvation Army Lt. Col. Ray Robinson braves wet weather to bring the Christmas spirit to San Francisco's Union Square.

Marilyn he ain't

While watching the Gay Freedom Day parade in San Francisco, this spectator becomes a participant when he discovers a rush of air rising from a sidewalk grating.

NEWSPAPER PHOTOGRAPHER OF THE YEAR, STEVEN RINGMAN, SAN FRANCISCO CHRONICLE

ROBBIE BEDELL, THE MIAMI HERALD

JEFF GREENE, THE JOURNAL (LORAIN, OHIO)

Above, a painter takes a lunch break while painting the St. Anastasia School in Fort Pierce, Fla.

Below, it's all a matter of perspective as Ann Skiver and Bill Weld wait for the start of a jazz concert in Pittsburgh's Point State Park.

Above, a bright sunny day, a good book, and a good window to take advantage of: prerequisites for a lazy spring day in Piqua, Ohio.

DAVID SPENCER, THE SUN-TATTLER (HOLLYWOOD, FLA.)

RECREATION

JOHN DUNN, JOURNAL INQUIRER (MANCHESTER, CONN.)

Above, a firefighter in Manchester, Conn., crawls into the attic of a burning home in an effort to avoid fumes from the blaze.

Below, a firefighter in Racine, Wis., goes into a small attic window to put a line on a fire caused by faulty electrical wiring.

CHARLES S. VALLONE, THE JOURNAL TIMES (RACINE, WIS.)

JIM GEHRZ, WORTHINGTON (MINN.) DAILY GLOBE

Above, in Fulda, Minn., 4-year-old Sarah Beckman finds the family pet, Toby, has a mind of its own.

JEFF ALEXANDER, THE ALBUQUERQUE (N.M.) JOURNAL

Above, 2-year-old Crystall England leads, kind of, the world's smallest horse, Tiny Tina, before an appearance at New Mexico's State Fair.

Right, Latonia Price gets a taste of victory as she finishes second in a junior Olympics sprint race in Grand Rapids, Mich.

LANCE WYNN, THE GRAND RAPIDS (MICH.) PRESS

MARK COURTNEY, THE POST-CRESCENT (APPLETON, WIS.)

Right, two Lawrence University students rig up a buddy system to mow lawns on the steep campus at Appleton, Wis.

Left, supervisors take the point and the rear to bring their roped-up charges back from a picnic at Point State Park, Pittsburgh.

ANDY STARNES, THE PITTSBURGH PRESS

Left, Toronto Blue Jay center fielder Lloyd Moseby removes toilet paper from Boston's Fenway Park after fans disagreed with the umpire's call.

Below, 4-year-old Randy Patterson of Framingham, Mass., ponders the next move in his dilemma.

WILLIAM POLO, THE BOSTON HERALD

CHRISTOPHER FITZGERALD, MIDDLESEX NEWS (FRAMINGHAM, MASS.)

G. LOIE GROSSMAN, PHILADELPHIA DAILY NEWS

DAVID RYAN, THE BOSTON GLOBE

J. CARL GANTER, THE COURIER-JOURNAL AND LOUISVILLE (KY.) TIMES

Upper left, Michael Jann, an ad agency employee, takes advantage of an available lap in Philadelphia's Logan Circle while he eats lunch on a warm March day.

Upper right, a worker gets a foothold on the statue of Revolutionary War Gen. John Glover on Boston's Commonwealth Avenue mall.

Right, Joshua Grace, 9, becomes part of history as he plays on a monument at Fort Harrod State Park in Harrodsburg, Ky. That's Daniel Boone Josh is leaning on.

Above, Alice spreads sheltering arms over wet weather drop-ins at her New York Wonderland.

FRED R. CONRAD, THE NEW YORK TIMES

Below, when students at the University of Louisville tried to compel school officials to abandon their policy of investing in companies doing business in South Africa, they enlisted a replica of Auguste Rodin's statue, "The Thinker," in their cause.

DURELL HALL, JR., THE COURIER-JOURNAL AND LOUISVILLE (KY.) TIMES

In Portland, Ore., just one more line of commuters on their way to work: elephants from the Ringling Brothers, Barnum & Bailey Circus.

MILAN CHUCKOVICH, THE COLUMBIAN (VANCOUVER, WASH.)

Right, in Indianapolis, two junior members of the Carson & Barnes Circus get all wound up in their act.

Below, in San Antonio, Texas, it's a long stretch for a peanut.

ROB GOEBEL, INDIANAPOLIS (IND.) STAR

CHUCK BECKLEY, SAN ANTONIO (TEXAS) LIGHT

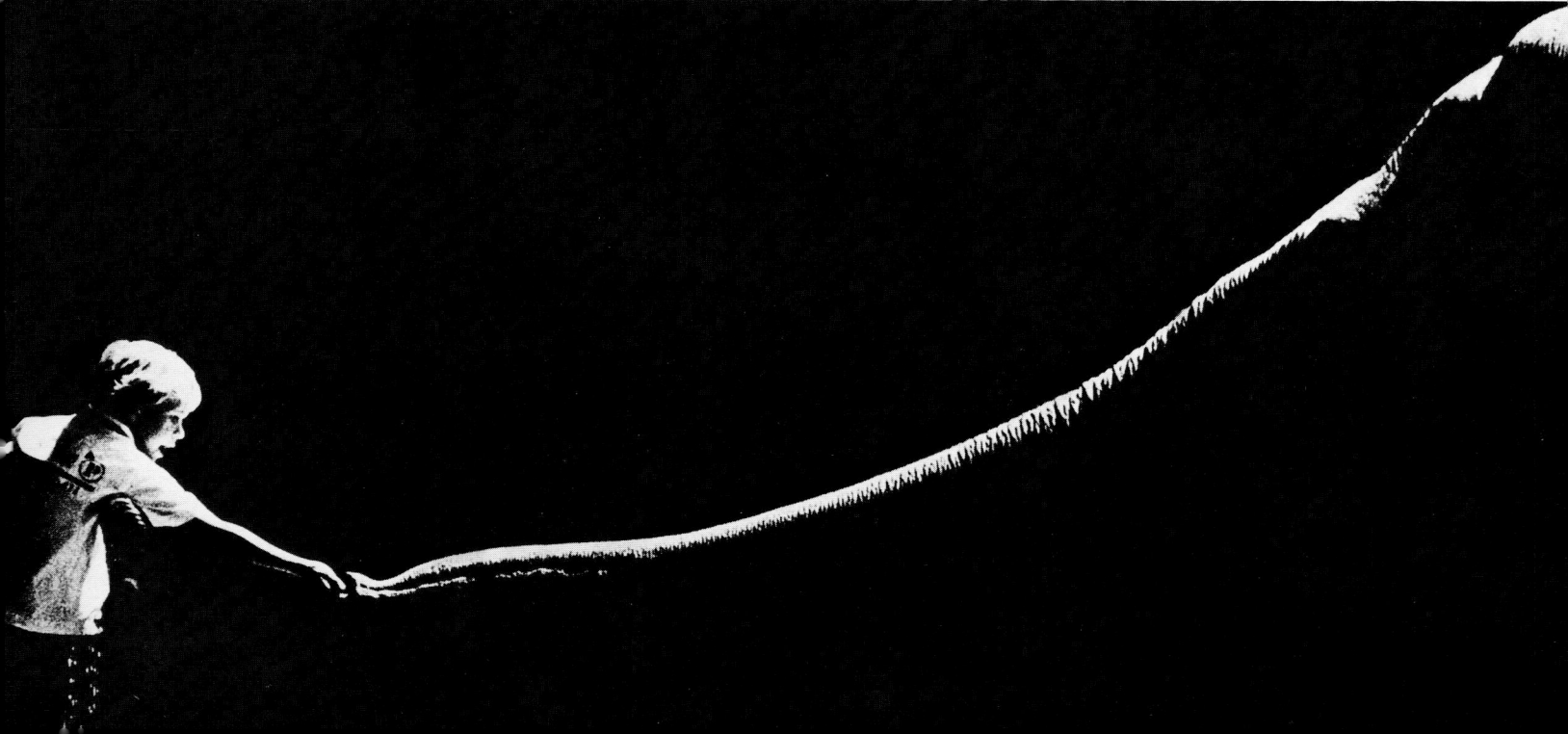

COLE PORTER, THE SEATTLE TIMES

In Seattle, a youngster offers friendship (and a handful of grass) to one of the residents of the Woodland Park Zoo.

JOHN EGGITT, REUTERS

In Chessington, England, a zookeeper takes the problem of parking Bella the elephant into her own hands.

SECOND PLACE NEWSPAPER HUMOR, GEORGE WILHELM, SIMI VALLEY (CALIF.) ENTERPRI

RICARDO J. FERRO, ST. PETERSBURG (FLA.) TIM

Above, just because there's a meet scheduled in this mallard's swimming pool is no reason for the duck to leave — not as long as it can keep ahead of the competition.

Right, sometimes it's more important to stay cool than to look pretty. This baby opossum cools off in a St. Petersburg animal shelter.

ALAN BERNER, THE SEATTLE TIMES

No go

It's supposed to be a takeoff. But this grebe can't get off the ground at Grays Harbor near Hoquiam, Wash.

Karen's boot camp

Dr. Karen Richter, 26, is a first-year resident doctor specializing in obstetrics and gynecology in San Francisco. Here, she winds up a month on rotation in the 15th-floor intensive care nursery, a job that is both mentally and physically demanding.

Richter's duty in the nursery includes delivering babies and caring for premature infants. She often works a 24-hour shift with little or no sleep: all part of a new physician's rigorous boot camp.

Right, dressed down in operating room, Richter waits and watches.

Below, Richter props herself against a wall during rounds with other residents.

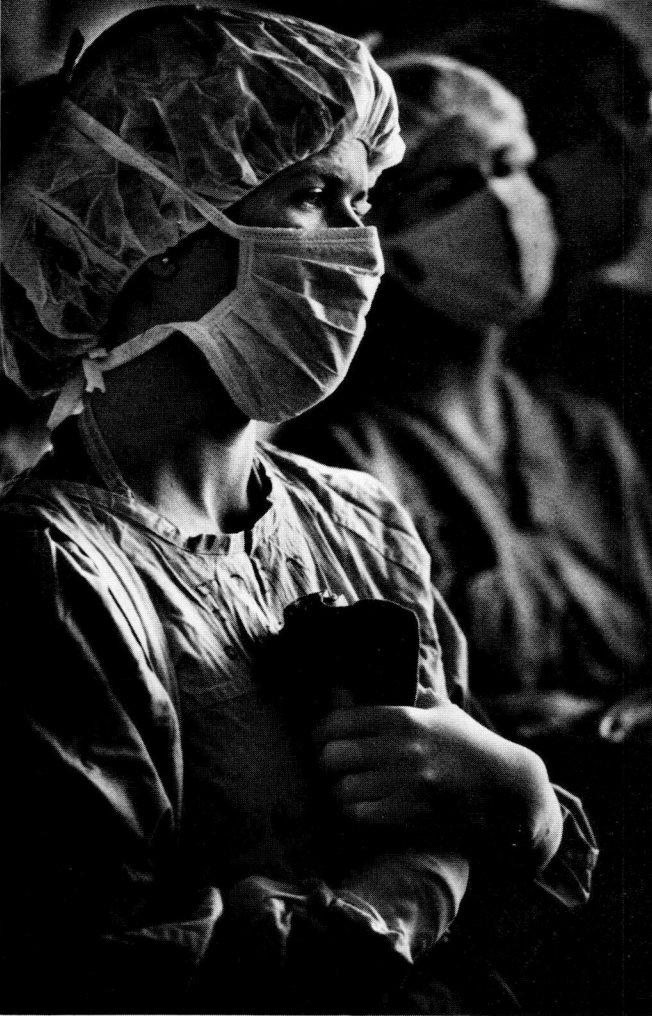

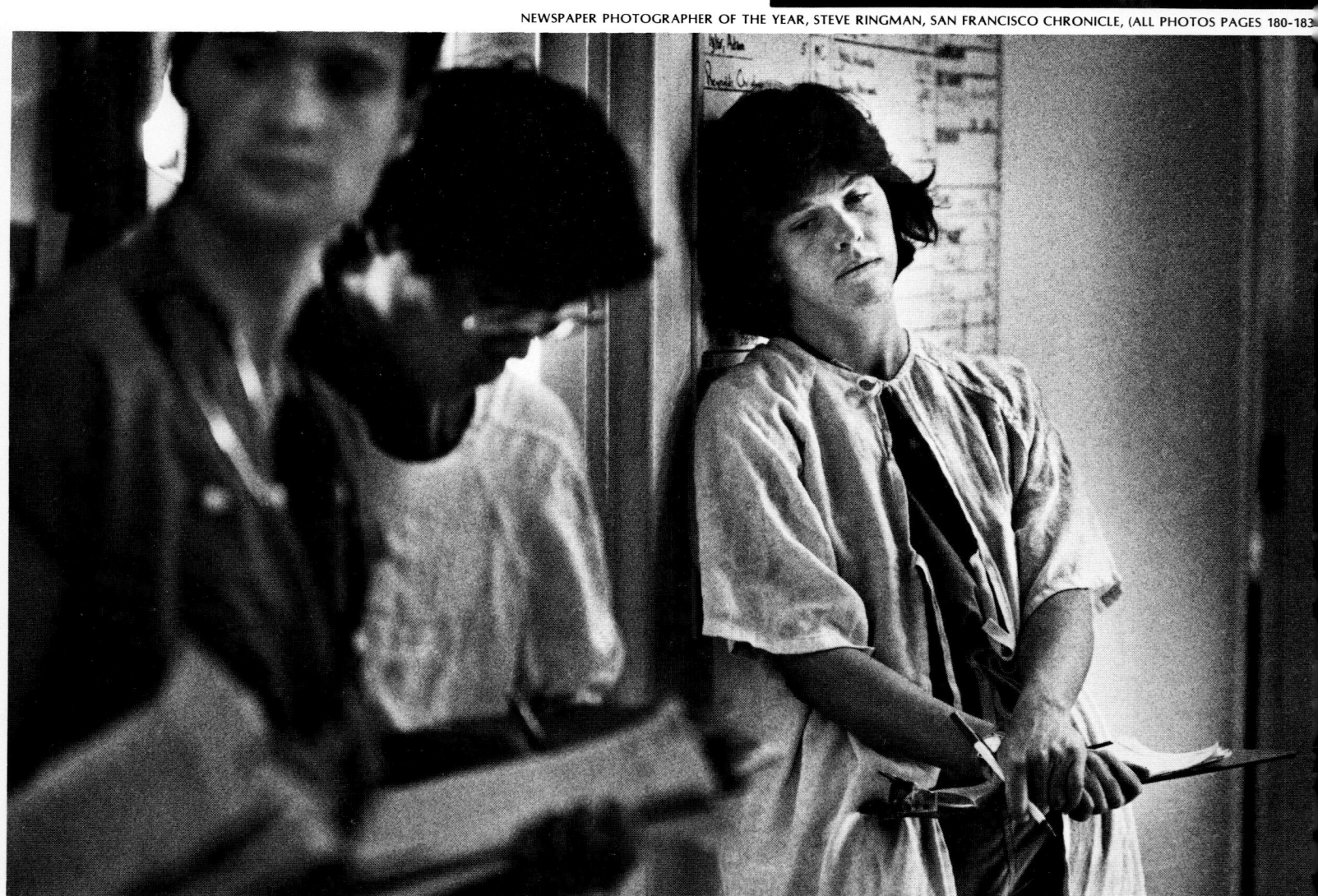

NEWSPAPER PHOTOGRAPHER OF THE YEAR, STEVE RINGMAN, SAN FRANCISCO CHRONICLE, (ALL PHOTOS PAGES 180-183)

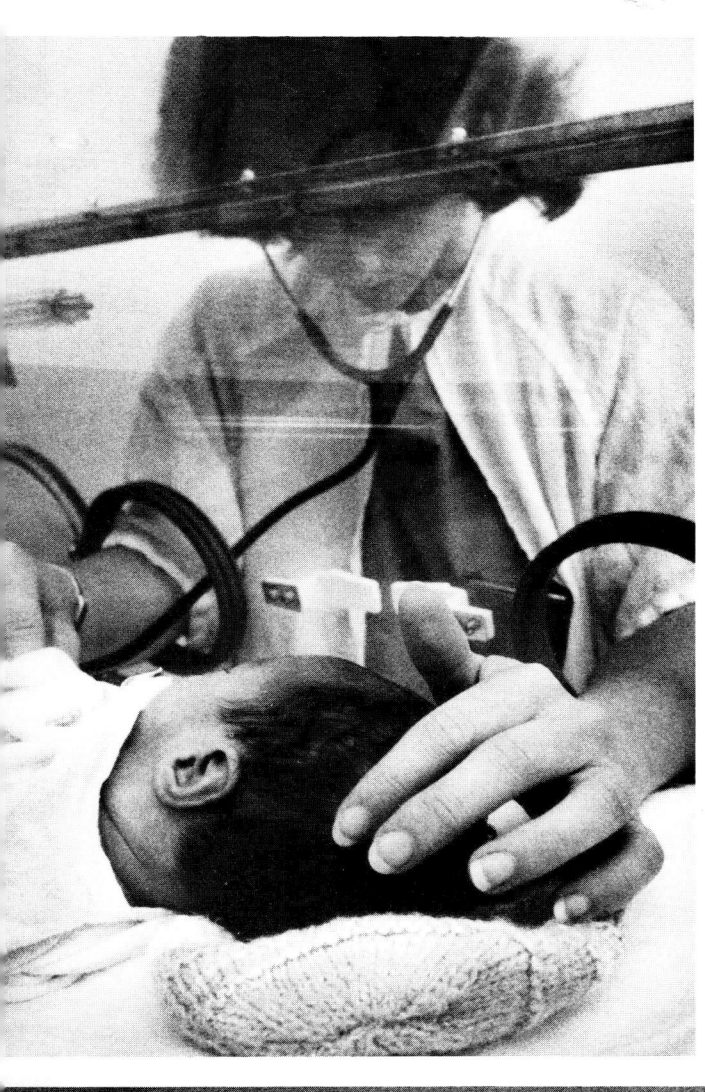

Left, Richter checks condition of a new patient.

Below, during a circuit of the patients, Richter is called to assist with an emergency caesarian section.

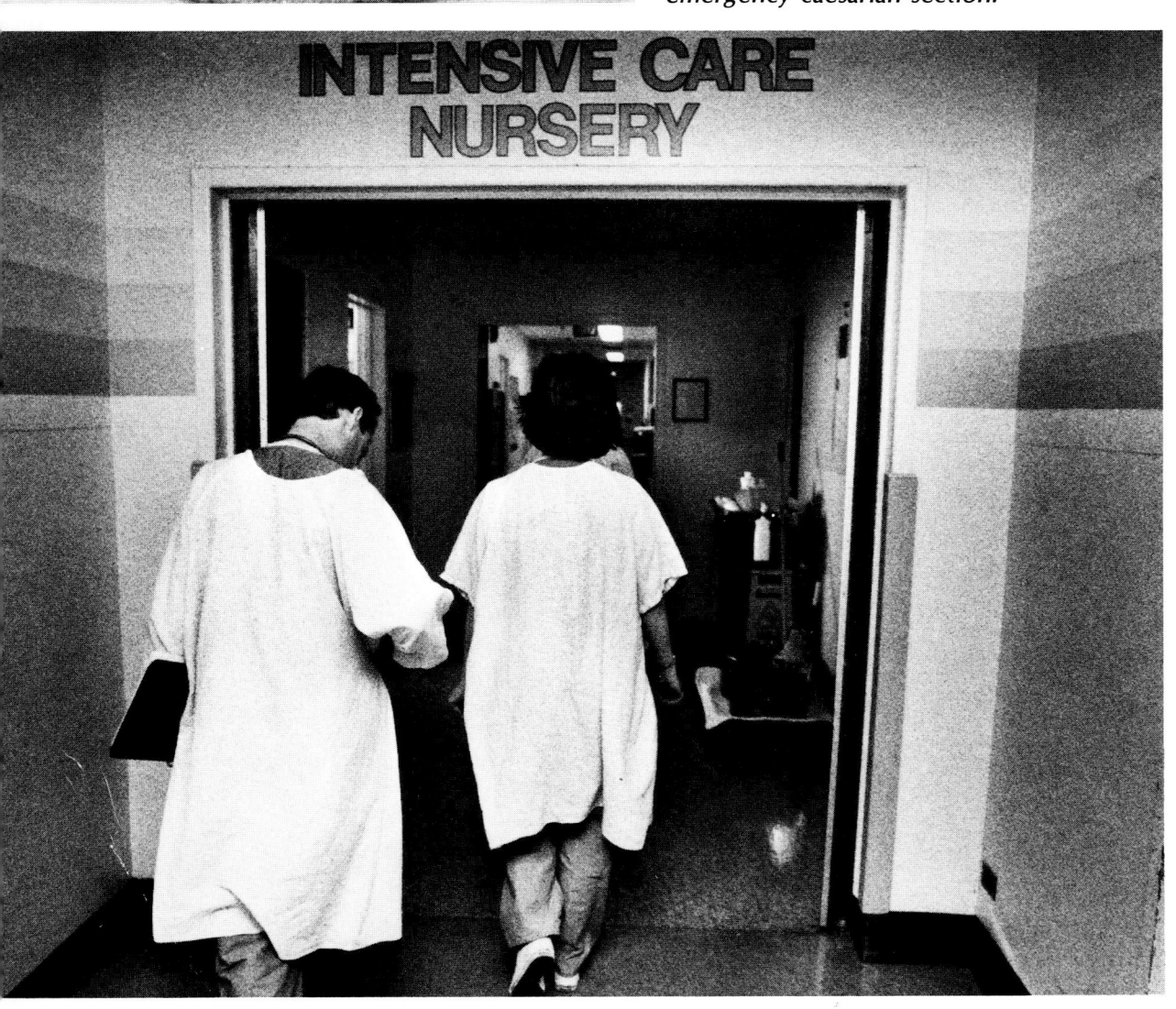

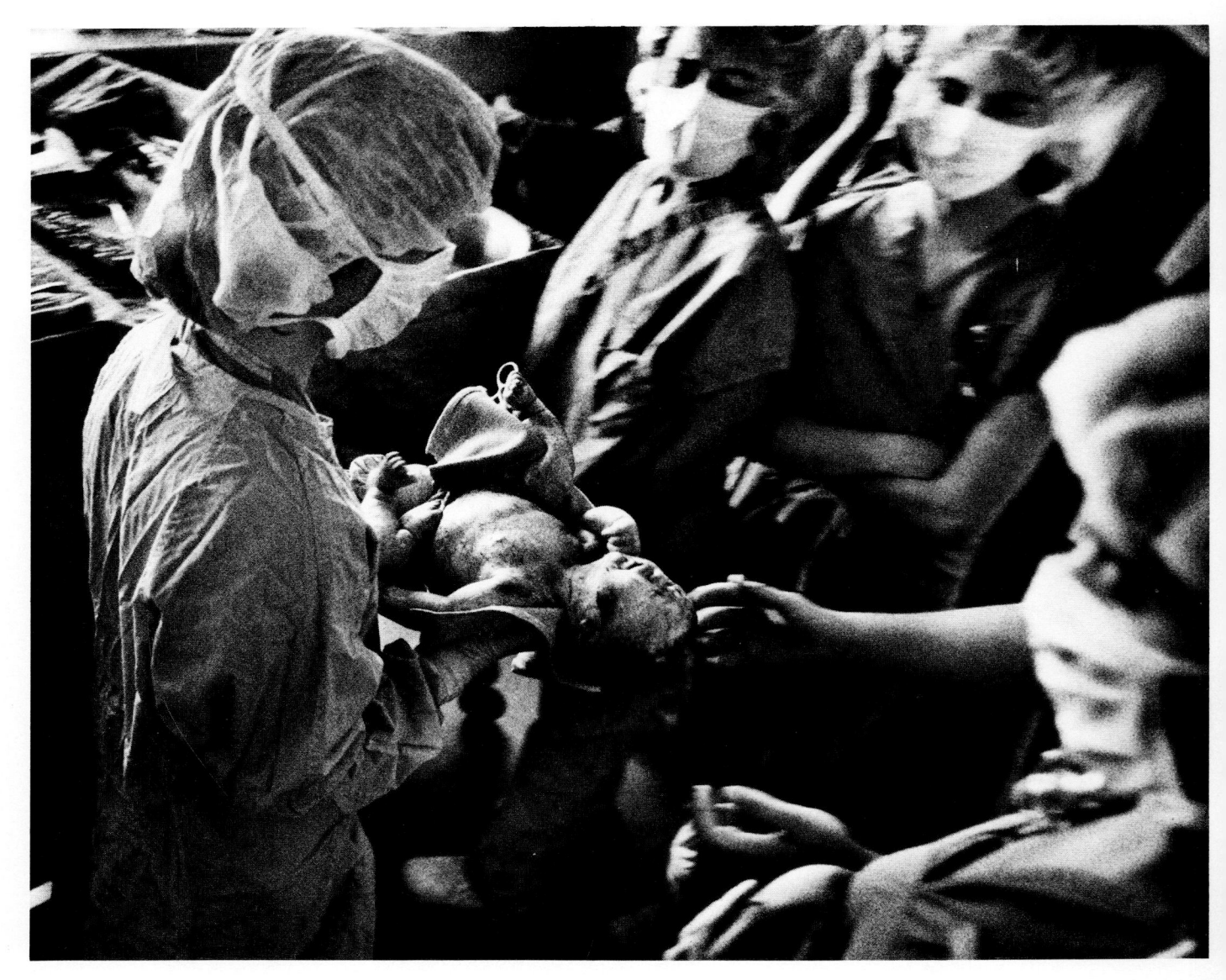

Boot camp

Above, seconds after a premature baby is born, he is placed in Richter's arms as she races toward intensive care nursery.

Right, only a third of the way into a 24-hour shift, Richter shows the strain of the work.

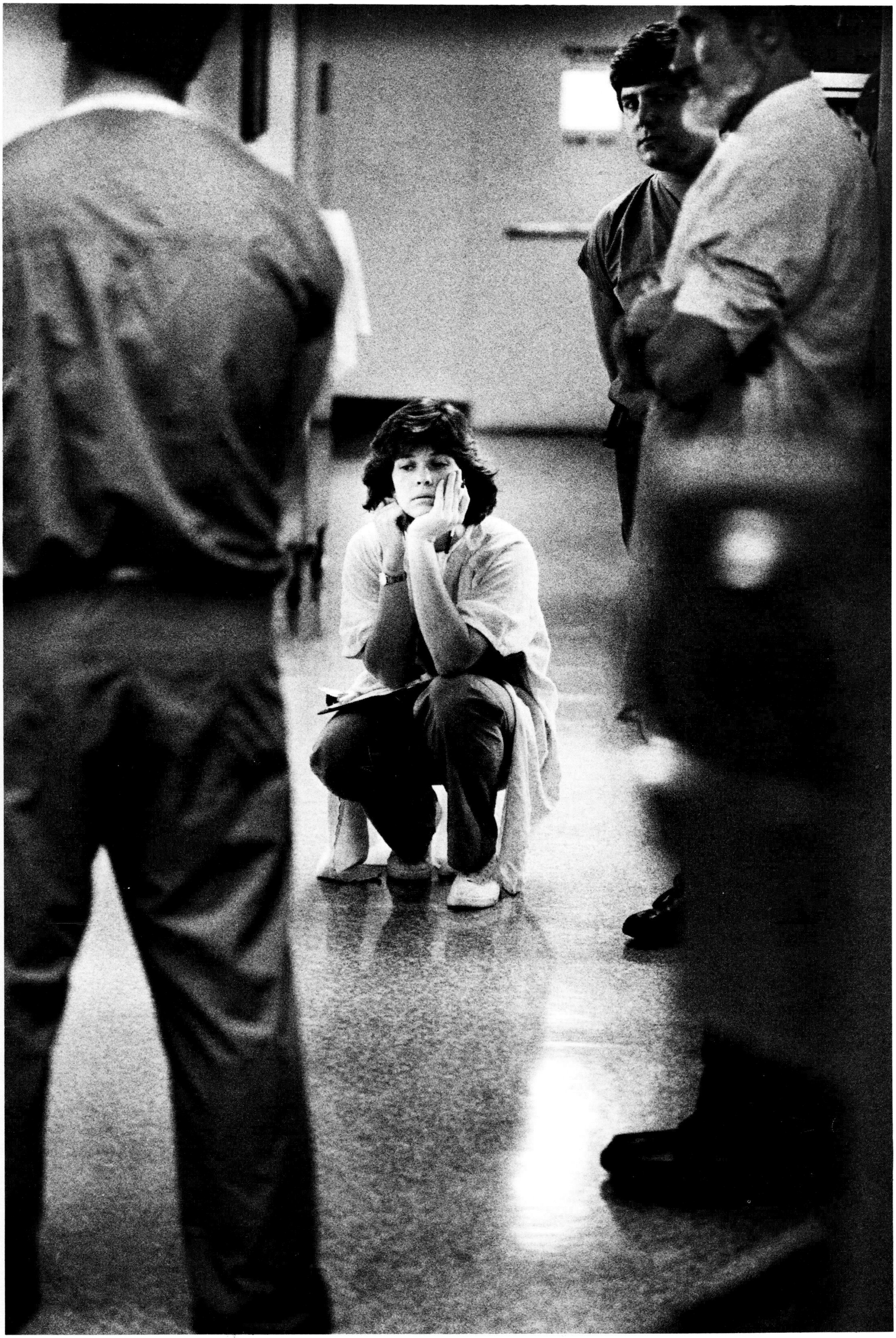

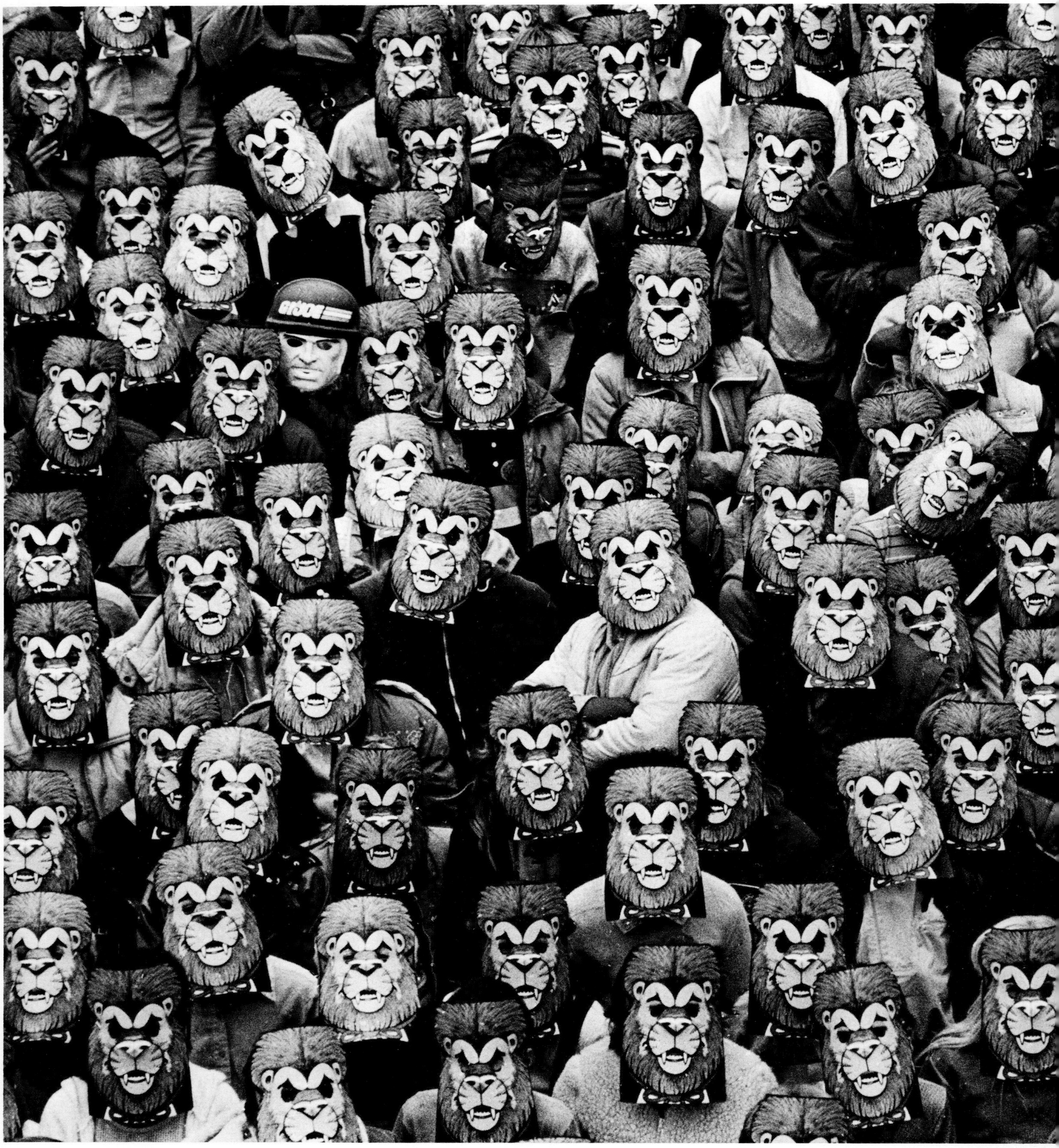
G.I.JOE

FRED COMEGYS, THE NEWS-JOURNAL, WILMINGTON, DEL.

More than 1,000 students from Calvin R. McCullough Elementary School in New Castle, Del., had a roaring good time when they donned lion masks and posed for this Halloween portrait. Guess what the school's mascot is?

JIM LARAGY, GANNETT ROCHESTER (N.Y.) NEWSPAPERS

Above, in Kendall, N.Y., Shirley Draper sells garden art that she makes in partnership with husband Paul. At $10 a copy, the Drapers were doing a brisk business.

Below, no doubt about it, Abe Rogers is trying to hitch a ride. Rogers, who says he is a citizen of Earth, is shown trying to get out of Sacramento, Calif.

RANDY PENCH, THE SACRAMENTO (CALIF.) BEE

ROBERT JORDAN, UNIVERSITY OF MISSISSIPPI

When wintry weather closed the University of Mississippi at Oxford in February, students used everything from inner tubes to garbage can lids to take advantage of the situation.

DENIS W. LAW, FLAHERTY NEWSPAPERS (SEATTLE, WASH.)

First snowfall of the year brought these three youngsters to one of Seattle's steepest hills. Two boys bloodied their noses in this maneuver, but were back on the hill within 10 minutes.

THIRD PLACE NEWSPAPER PHOTOGRAPHER OF THE YEAR, ERIC LUSE, SAN FRANCISCO CHRONIC

Above, fans of the San Francisco 49rs went crazy on Market Street after their team won the Super Bowl before a home town crowd. (No, number 42 is not a real 49r.)

Right, St. Louis Cardinal Jouquin Andujar is restrained by teammates during the seventh game of the World Series. Andujar got into an argument with the home plate umpire and was tossed out of the game. The Kansas City Royals won both the game and the Series.

RIGHT, FRANK NIEMEIR, THE KANSAS CITY (MO.) TIM

Sports scene —
Winners and losers

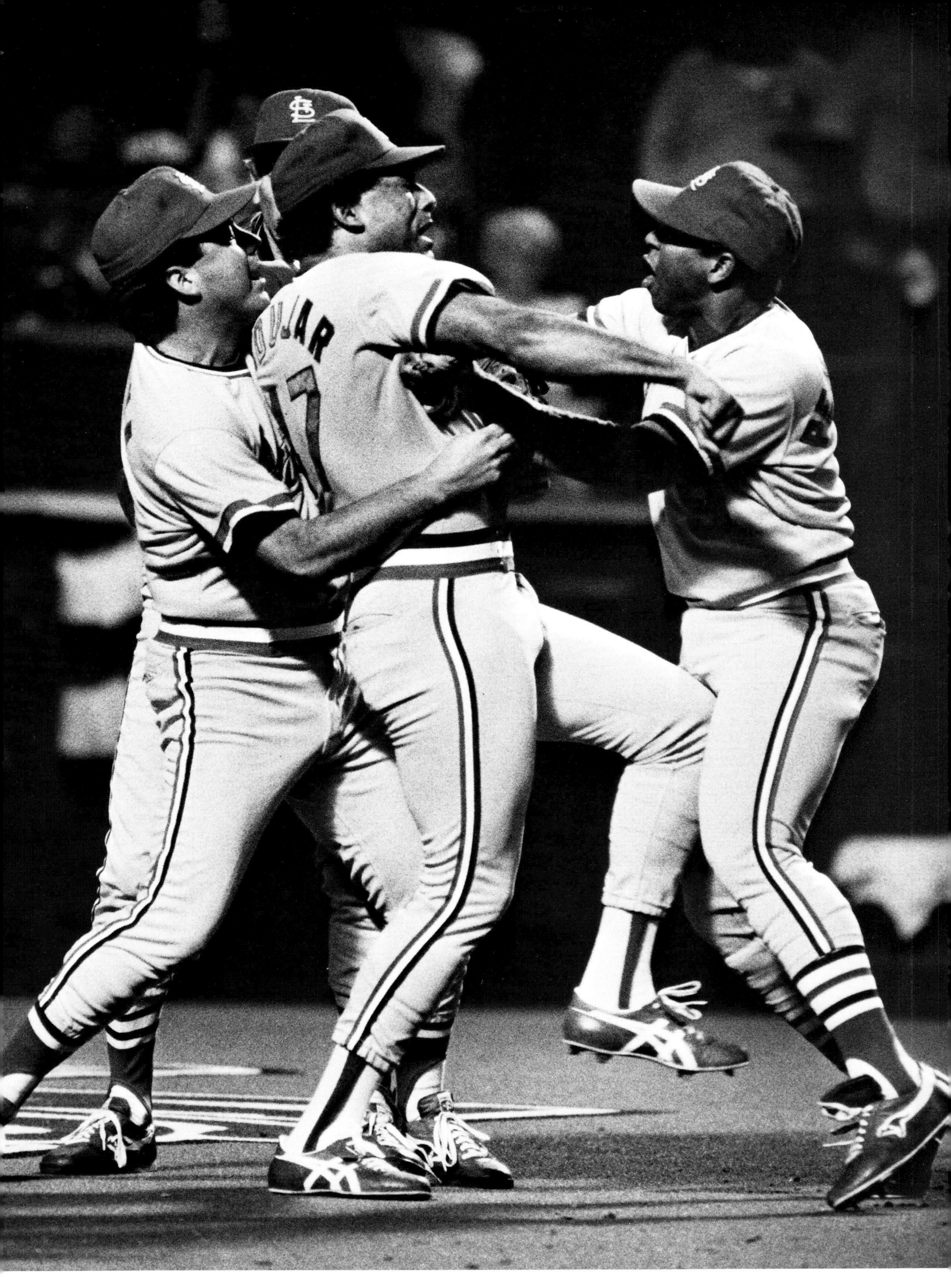

CHARLES F. EATON, JR., THE DAILY COURIER (FOREST CITY, N.C.)

BRIAN S. TOMBAUGH, THE JOURNAL (LORAIN, OHIO)

All the drama of The Game is caught in these two photographs: Infield play in North Carolina (left) and a hitter in Ohio (above). Only T-ball, perhaps, but photographer Charles F. Eaton, Jr., points out that it is "the first short step down the long road to professional baseball. And if you don't make it, who cares?"

The boys of summer

GREG PETERS, THE HUTCHINSON (KAN.) NEW

Above, Jennifer Harrison of the Del City, Okla., Zappers appeals to umpire Al Neely on a call at home plate during the Girls World Softball Tournament in Hutchinson, Kan. The Zappers won the call.

Below, Louisiana Little Leaguer Rusty Benoit waits for the umpire's call on his slide into second base: Safe.

TED JACKSON, THE TIMES-PICAYUNE PUBLISHING CORP. (NEW ORLEANS, LA

JAMES P. McCOY, NIAGARA GAZETTE (NIAGARA FALLS, N.Y.)

Above, "I'VE GOT IT!" says the outfield of Buckey's Barber Shop Hyde Park (N.Y.) Majors Little League baseball team as it warms up fielding flies.

Below, one policeman forgot he was on security duty when Vanderbilt's football team held onto a 7-0 lead to beat Tennessee Chattanooga in Nashville.

SECOND PLACE NEWSPAPER SPORTS FEATURE, RICK MANSFIELD, NASHVILLE (TENN.) BANNER

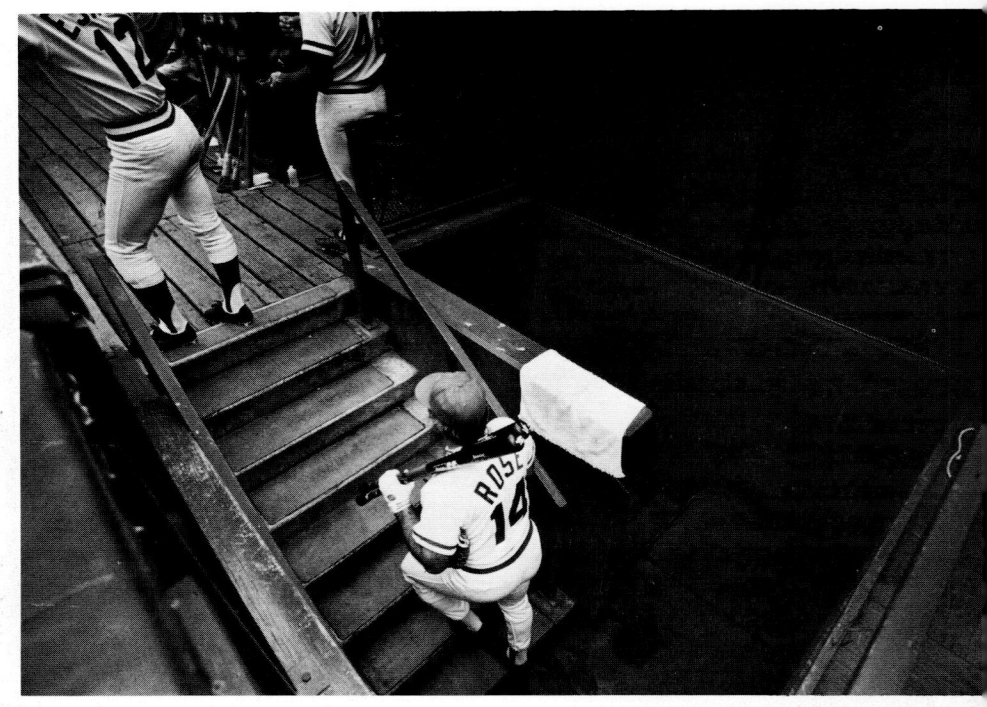

Right, armed with his weapons, Rose emerges, from the bowels of the stadium.

Below, before the game Pete Rose talks with reporters about his record pursuit. By this time, Rose was being followed by newsmen almost around the clock.

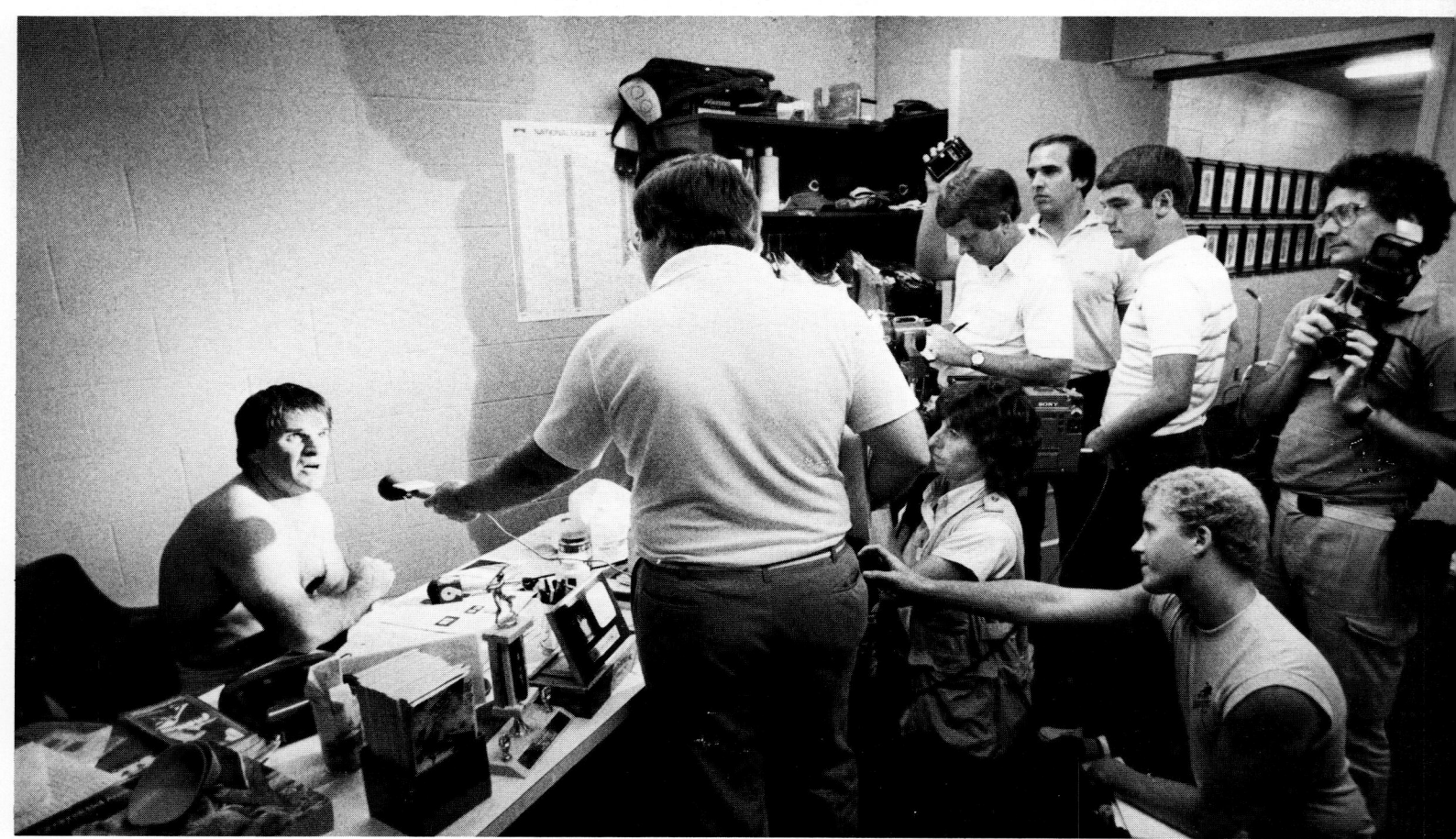

SECOND PLACE NEWSPAPER SPORTS PICTURE STORY, BILL FRAKES, THE MIAMI HERALD (ALL PHOTOS PAGES 194-1

'Bye-bye, Ty!'

For Cincinnati Reds fans, the 1985 season was Pete Rose's year, a time when the Reds' player manager chased the base hit record set so long ago by Ty Cobb.

The payoff came in Cincinnati's River Front Stadium Sept. 11. In a game against the San Diego Padres, one out, bottom of the first, Ros hit his 4,192nd base hit — and went into the record book.

Above, a determined Rose at the plate.

Left, a determined young fan at a smorgasbord of Rose souvenir items.

Next up, Number 14.

'Bye-bye, Ty!'

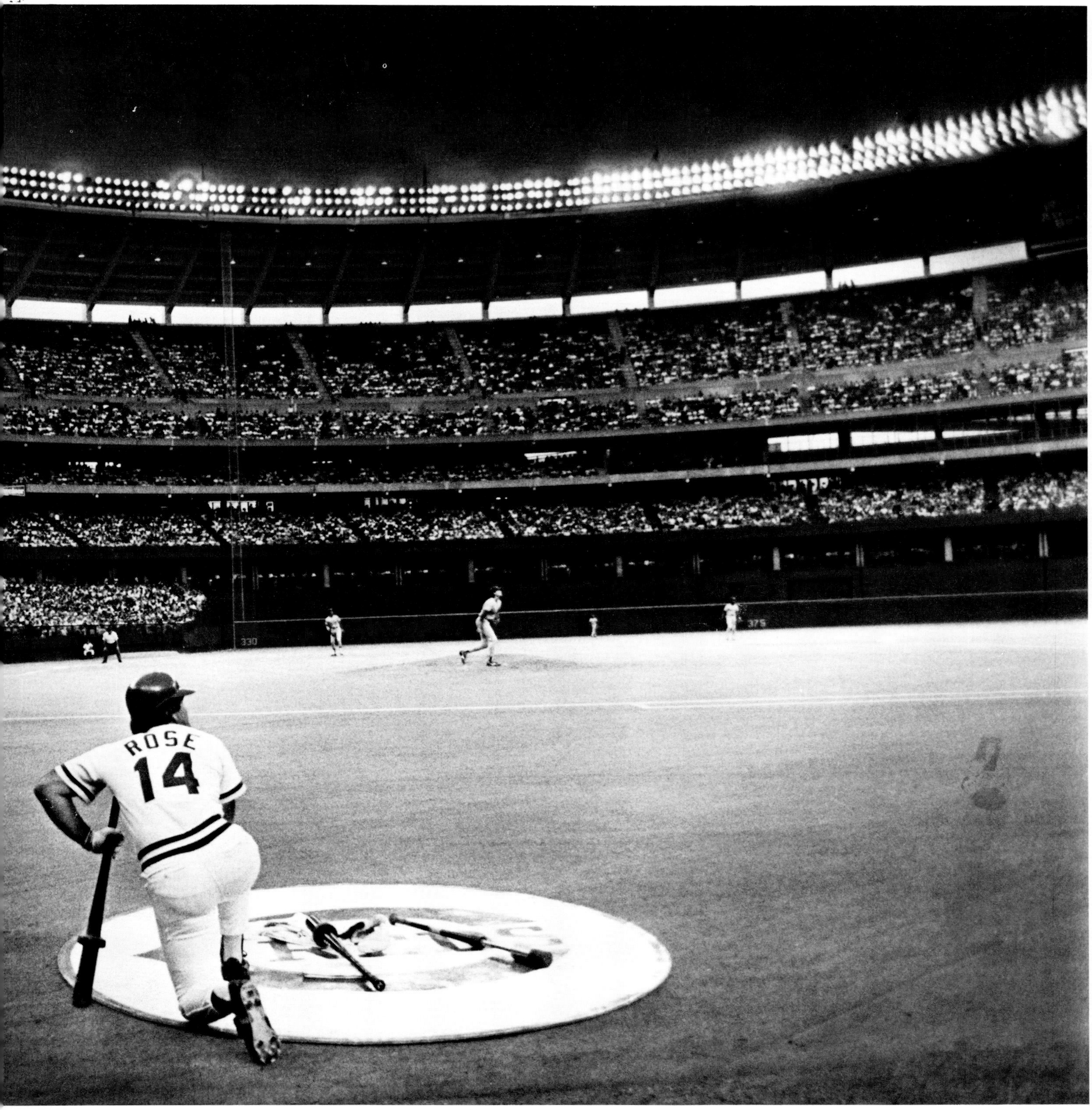
ROSE
14
330
375

Rose watches the hit that broke Ty Cobb's all-time record fall into short left field as the fans show their appreciation with cheers, signs, and confetti.

'Bye-bye, Ty.

Crying for the first time since his father died, Rose reacts to the culmination of his long, long chase.

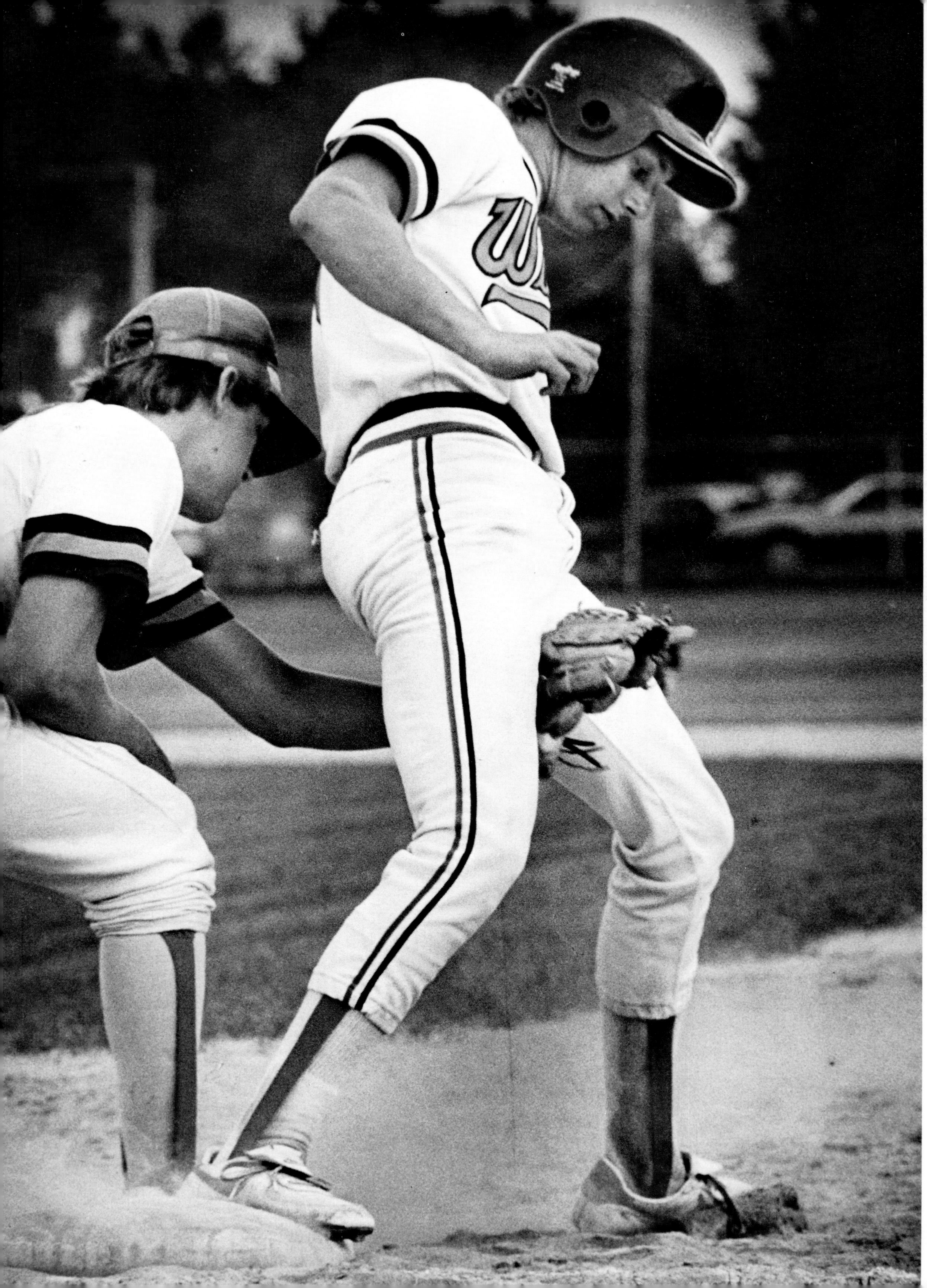

BRUCE BISPING, MINNEAPOLIS STAR AND TRIBUNE

PAUL CHINN, LOS ANGELES HERALD EXAMINER

Above, San Diego's Craig Nettles plays catch with sons Tim (left) and Jeff during All-Star game warm-up at Metrodome in Minneapolis.

Left, goofy glove work, all right; but infielder Mark Gunther is late with his tag as he tries to catch Darren Tyson in a suburban Chicago summer league game.

LEFT, JONATHAN KIRN, THE DAILY HERALD (ARLINGTON HEIGHTS, ILL.)

Above, San Francisco Giants infielder Jeff Leonard loses his cap as he avoids a sliding LA Dodger base runner, Ken Landreaux, in a game at Dodger Stadium.

Clutch play

Above, George Brett gives a lift to pitcher Bret Saberhagen as the Kansas City Royals win the World Series in their seventh game with the St. Louis Cardinals.

KEITH MYERS, THE KANSAS CITY (MO.) TIMES

Right, an exuberant Blue Jays fan in Toronto leaps onto the mound to grab pitcher Dave Stieb during first game of the American League playoffs.

RIGHT, BILL CREIGHTON, REUTERS

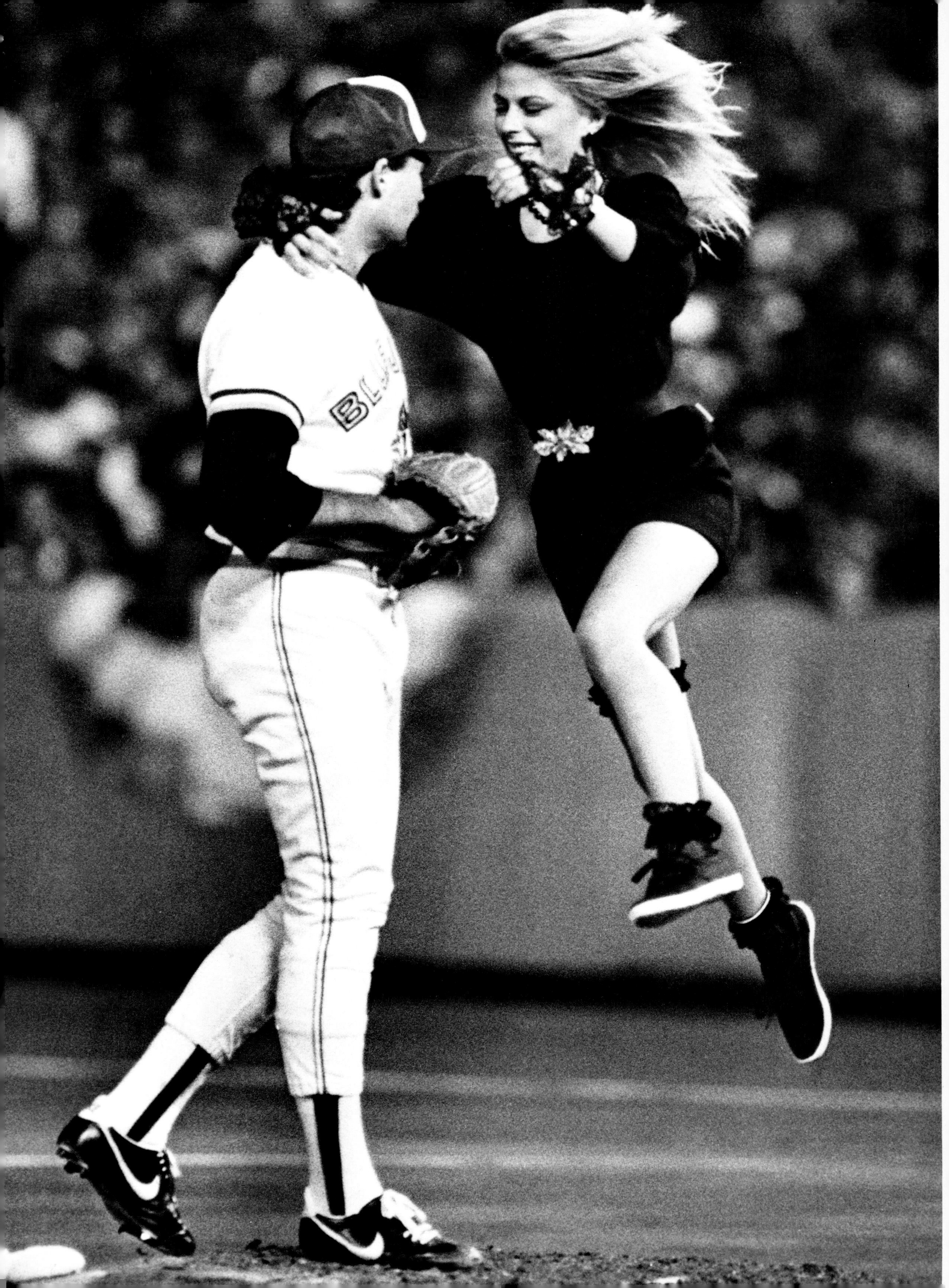

NEWSPAPER PHOTOGRAPHER OF THE YEAR STEVE RINGMAN, SAN FRANCISCO CHRONICLE

Above, San Francisco Giants players take time to go along with the music being broadcast at Candlestick Park.

Below, Nell Grim was the only woman among 60 base buffs to sign up for a week-long Mickey Mantle/Whitey Ford Yankee Fantasy Camp in St. Petersburg, Fla. Talk about a fantasy; talk about attention.

PAM SMITH O'HARA, THE MIAMI HERALD

NEWSPAPER PHOTOGRAPHER OF THE YEAR STEVE RINGMAN, SAN FRANCISCO CHRONICLE

Above, the look of a winner; San Francisco 49rs Coach Bill Walsch right after winning the Super Bowl.

Below, Toledo's Phil Foubert grimaces in pain after falling on the track during the steeplechase event at the Drake Relays in Des Moines.

DOUG WELLS, THE DES MOINES (IOWA) REGISTER

JIM MENDENHALL, THE ORANGE COUNTY REGISTER (SANTA ANA, CALIF.)

RONALD CORTES, THE NEWS-JOURNAL CO. (WILMINGTON, DE

Above, the Philadelphia Sixers' Dr. J isn't the young player he once was, but he shows the Chicago Bulls that he can still fly.

Left, Larry Bird and the Celtics are knocked out of the air by the Lakers in the fifth game of the National Basketball Assn. championship series. The Lakers won the title a game later.

Laker Center Kareem Abdul-Jabbar goes over Sam Bowie of the Portland Trailblazers with his Skyhook (which is helped by that strong left elbow).

JAMES RUEBSAMEN, LOS ANGELES HERALD EXAMINER

STEVE NESIUS, GAINESVILLE (FLA.) SUN

Virginia Tech football players go four deep on a fumble by the University of Florida. Florida won the game, nonetheless.

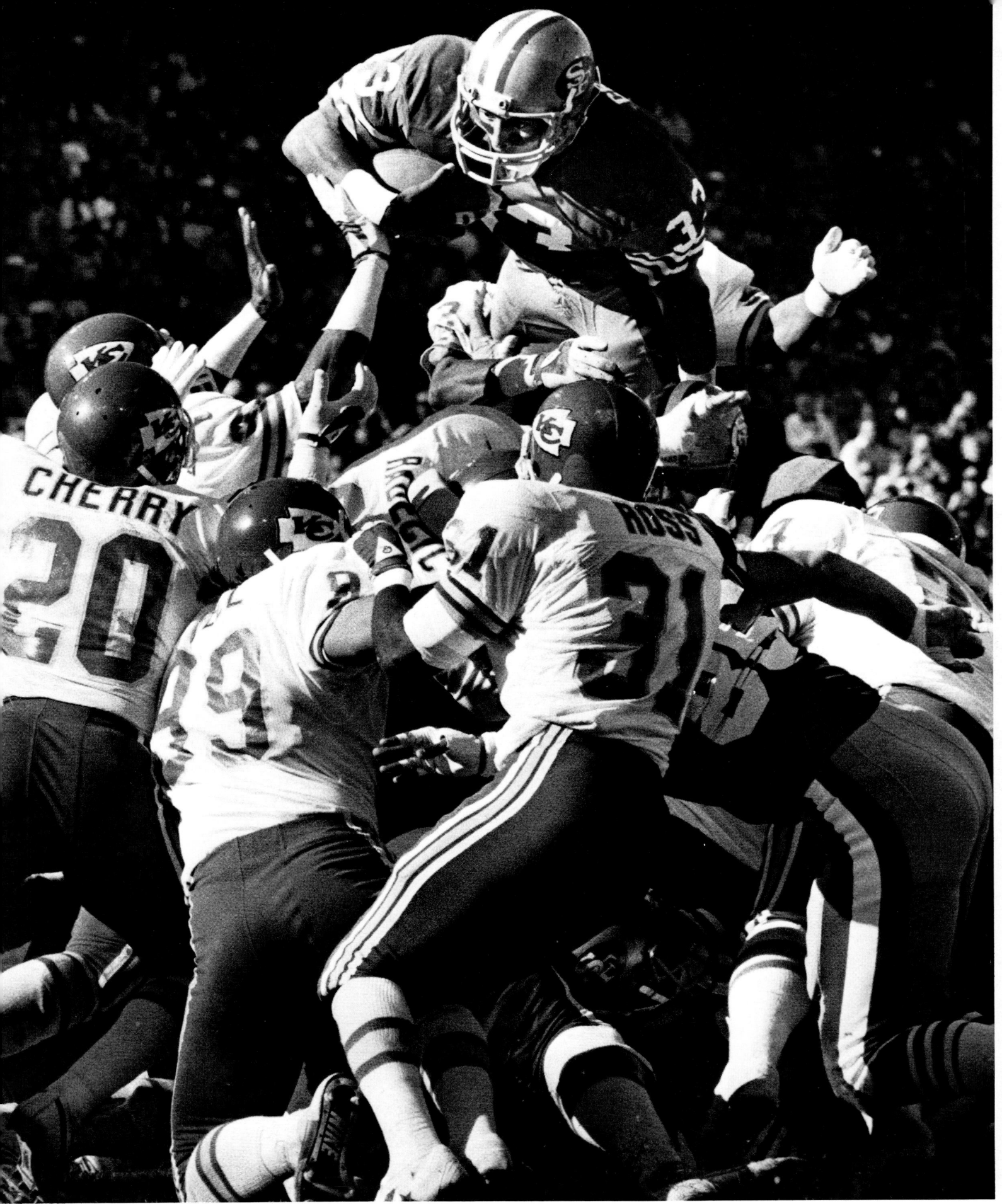

CHRIS STEWART, SAN FRANCISCO CHRONICLE

oger Craig of the San Francisco 49rs goes
ver the top for a touchdown during a game
ith the Kansas City Chiefs.

FIRST PLACE NEWSPAPER SPORTS PICTURE STORY, FRED COMEGYS, THE NEWS-JOURNAL CO. (WILMINGTON, DEL.) (ALL PHOTOS PAGES 210-21

Above, Middies went to midfield before the game started to give Army the big fingers.

Navy's day

For cadets from West Point and midshipmen from Annapolis, a December afternoon in Philadelphia was the focal point of the 1985 athletic year. And when the 86th game in the Army-Navy gridiron series ended, Navy had upset Army 17-7.

Among Navy heroes: Napoleon McCallum, who set a number of NCAA records while bowling over Army defenders. Said McCallum: "Of all the games ... this is the greatest one right here."

The rest of the Annapolis contingent agreed. The cadets? Well, wait until next year.

Above, Navy's Napoleon McCallum breaks through the Army line. He gained more than 200 yards rushing in Navy's upset victory.

Above, one midshipman apparently has something else on his mind.

Left, Middies lose their cool — and their clothes — as victory seems certain.

Go, Navy

Right, Navy enthusiasm peaks as time runs out for Army.

Below, Navy's McCallum gets a victory ride off the field from fellow midshipmen.

Left, an exuberant Middie leaps into the arms of nose guard Dave Pimpo.

Below, two Naval Academy players savor their victory as midshipmen gather on the field at Veterans Stadium to sing the Navy Hymn after the game.

THIRD PLACE NEWSPAPER PORTRAIT/PERSONALITY, LANCE WYNN, THE GRAND RAPIDS (MICH.) PRESS

Above, boxer Thomas Hearns at the end of a sparring session, preparing for a middleweight fight with Marvin Hagler.

Right, Marvelous Marvin Hagler is hoisted high by his trainers after scoring a decisive third-round knockout against Thomas Hearns in April in Las Vegas. It was Hagler's 51st knockout.

JIM LAURIE, LAS VEGAS (NEV.) REVIEW-JOURN

JAMES RUEBASMEN, LOS ANGELES HERALD EXAMINER

Ruben Castillo gets comfort and consolation from his trainer after he was knocked out by Julio Cesar Chavez in the Inglewood, Calif., Forum.

Heavyweight Larry Holmes was behind on points in the 15th round of his championship fight with challenger Michael Spinks. Here he's getting psyched by trainer Richie Giachetti. But Holmes lost the fight, and his crown.

WAYNE C. KODEY, LAS VEGAS (NEV.) REVIEW-JOURNAL

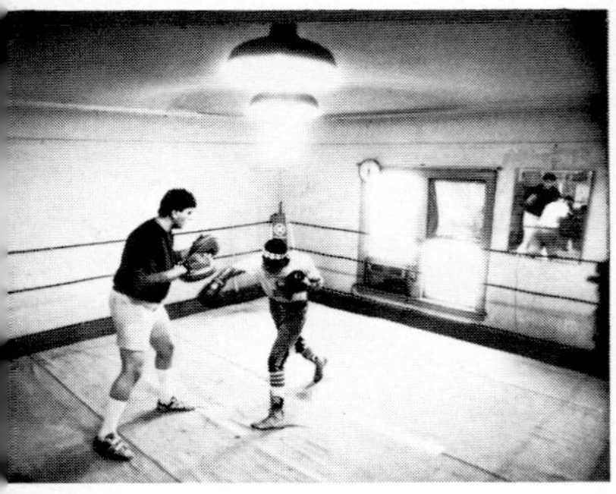

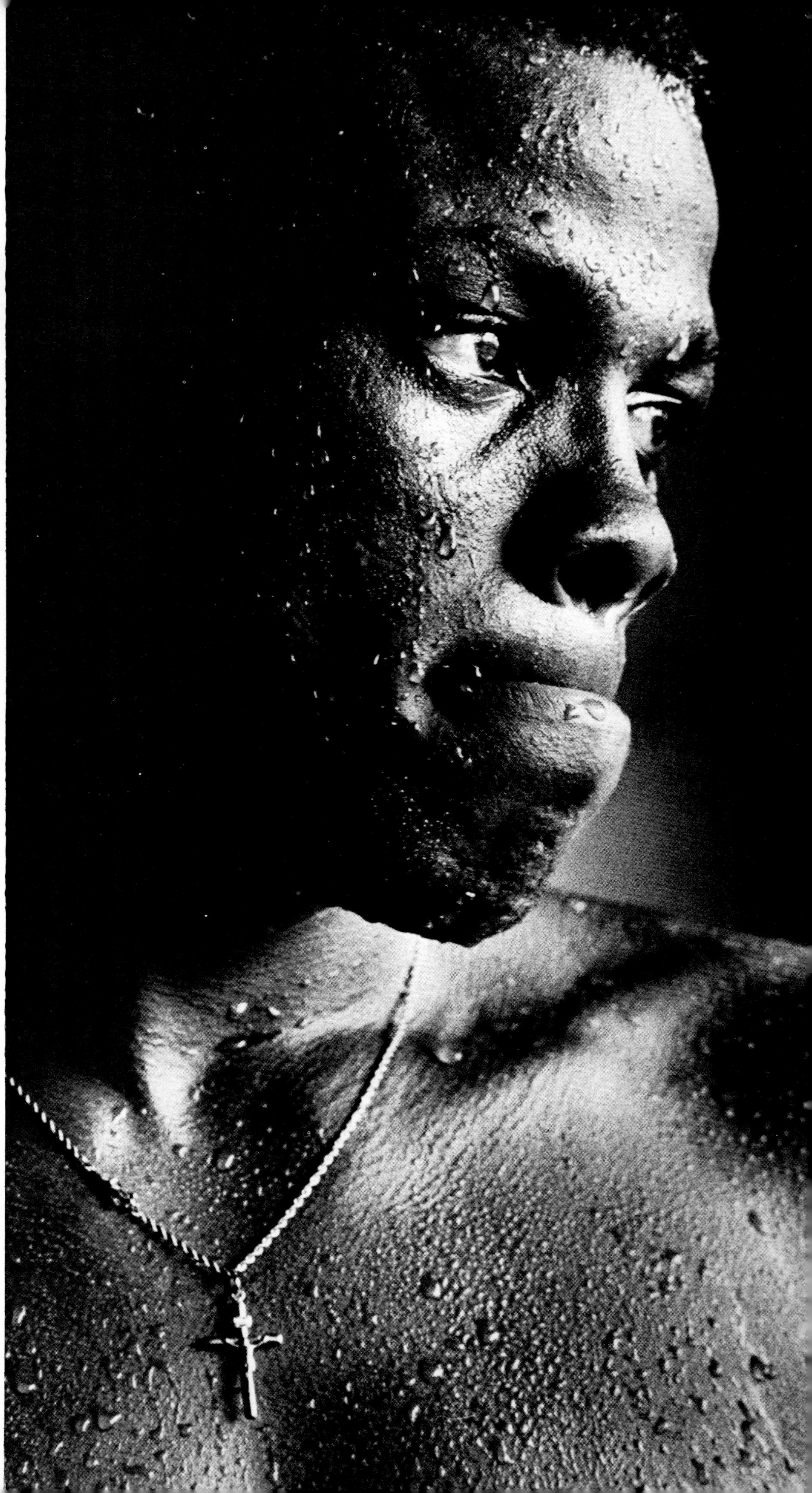

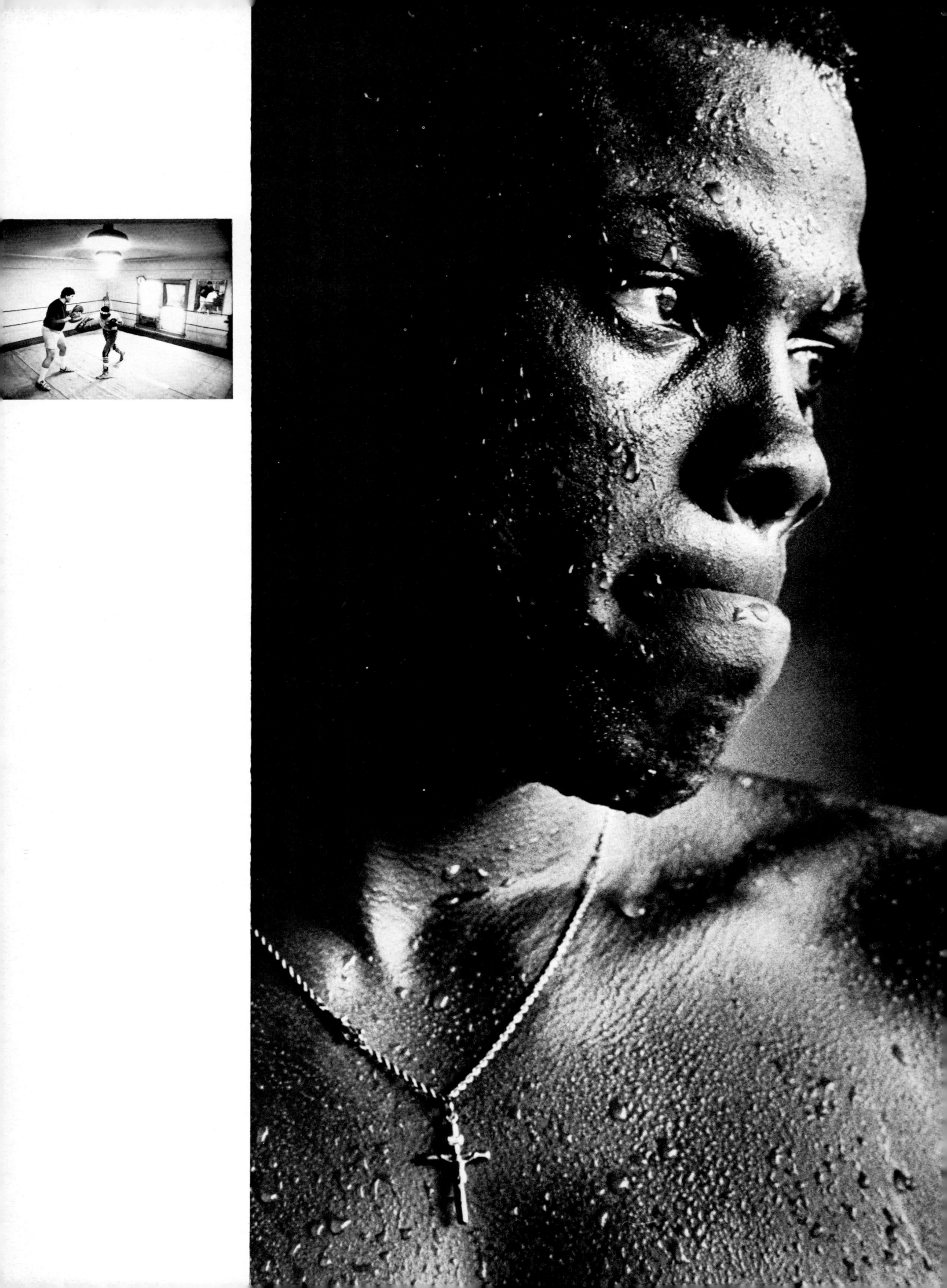

THIRD PLACE NEWSPAPER SPORTS PICTURE STORY, LUI KIT WONG, SAN JOSE (CALIF.) MERCURY NEWS (ALL PHOTOS PAGES 216-219)

A glove and a prayer

Mitchell Julien lost a fight he was expected to win on his way to the junior welterweight boxing crown. It turned his life around.

"I know now I have an objective, and I know what I have to accomplish," the young Palo Altoan says.

The boxer's past includes trouble with the law and a refusal to get serious about training. But after the upset he took stock, decided to settle down - and start back up the junior welterweight ladder.

Above, Mitchell works on his speed on a timing bag and (right) toughens his neck muscles upside down against the ropes.

Glove, prayer

Above, Mitchell takes a break after a workout in 105-degree heat. Left below, Mitchell's trainer, Jeff Grmoja, keeps the pressure on his boxer. Right below, Mitchell takes time before a bout to pray for the safety of his opponent and himself.

Above, an opponent prepares to take the force of Mitchell's punch.

Below, Mitchell celebrates after scoring a second-round knockout.

MARK B. SLUDER, THE CHARLOTTE (N.C.) OBSERVER

BILL TIERNAN, THE VIRGINIAN-PILOT/LEDGER-STAR (NORFOLK)

Above, Bobby Ginsberg successfully takes State Hill over a jump at the U.S. Open Horse Jumping Championships in Charlotte, N.C.

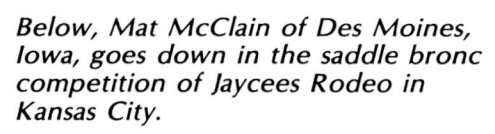

Below, Mat McClain of Des Moines, Iowa, goes down in the saddle bronc competition of Jaycees Rodeo in Kansas City.

Above, a modern knight drives toward a one-inch target during Natural Chimneys 164th annual Jousting Tourney in Mount Solon, Va.

THIRD PLACE NEWSPAPER SPORTS ACTION, CHRIS STEWART, FREELANCE FOR THE KANSAS CITY (MO.) TIMES

DAN ROOT, MISSOULIAN (MISSOULA, MONT.)

Above, victory is sweet for Emma Briscoe. The only woman to enter track and field events at the Missoula, Mont., Senior Games, the 71-year-old won both 50-and 100-meter dashes.

ALLEN EYESTONE, THE PALM BEACH (FLA.) POST-TIMES

SECOND PLACE NEWSPAPER PHOTOGRAPHER OF THE YEAR, JOHN KAPLAN, THE PITTSBURGH PRESS

Above, Ken and Lisa Martin made sports history, winning both male and female divisions in a major race, the Pittsburgh Marathon. The couple from Mesa, Ariz., pocketed $55,000 in prize money.

Left, Bill Weinacht, 69 (left), edges Don Hull, 66, in the 220-yard dash during the Second Wind Track and Field Championships in Lake Worth, Fla. Weinacht won six gold medals and the overall championship for ages 65-69

221

GEORGE REYNOLDS, PHILADELPHIA DAILY NEWS
Tennis player Mel Percell shows his displeasure with a linesman's call at the U.S. Indoor Tennis Championships in Philadelphia. (No harm done.)

Above, Martina Navratilova reacts to the ball's dropping over the net to score a point against Sandra Cecchini in the third round of the U.S. Open Tennis Championship. Navratilova beat her opponent in just 37 minutes.

MARK VERGARI, GANNETT WESTCHESTER (N.Y.) NEWSPAPERS

Below, John McEnroe kicks at a television camera that he felt got too close during finals of U.S. Pro Indoor meet. McEnroe won the tourney anyhow.

AMY SANCETTA, ASSOCIATED PRESS

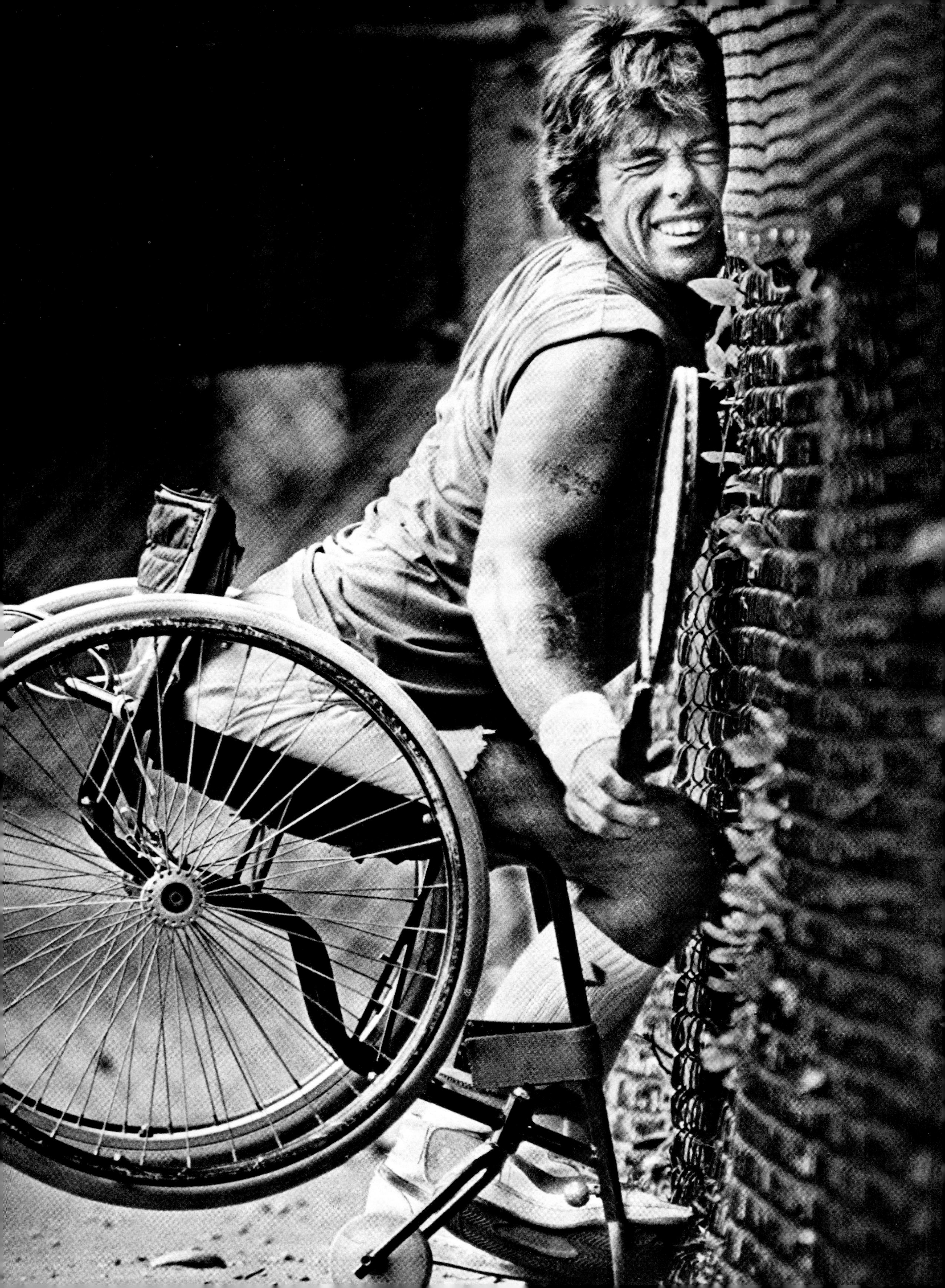

FIRST PLACE NEWSPAPER SPORTS ACTION, JOHN BLANDING, THE BOSTON GLOBE
GUY REYNOLDS, MORNING ADVOCATE (BATON ROUGE, LA.)

Above, Biker Brian Griffith tumbles over a fallen Ed Bernasky in Mayor's Cup Races in Salem, Mass.

Right, Betsy King rides alone, far ahead of the pack, in the 70-kilometer women's road race at the National Sports Festival in Baton Rouge, La.

eft, John Johnston, number-one anked wheelchair tennis player in lorida, smashes into the side oundary fence while chasing a ackhand volley. Johnston, who was njured in Vietnam, has been playing ennis seven years.

EFT, SECOND PLACE NEWSPAPER SPORTS ACTION, BILL WAX, THE GAINESVILLE (FLA.) SUN

WILLIAM H. BATSON, OMAHA (NEB.) WORLD-HERALD

Goalpost goes over at the University of Oklahoma in Norman, after the Sooners beat the Nebraska Cornhuskers, 27-7.

An injured soccer fan is carried to safety after a stand wall collapsed just before the start of the European Cup finals between Great Britain and Italy in Brussels. Rampaging British fans turned the event into a bloody battle; 38 persons were killed.

NICK DIDLICK, REUTERS

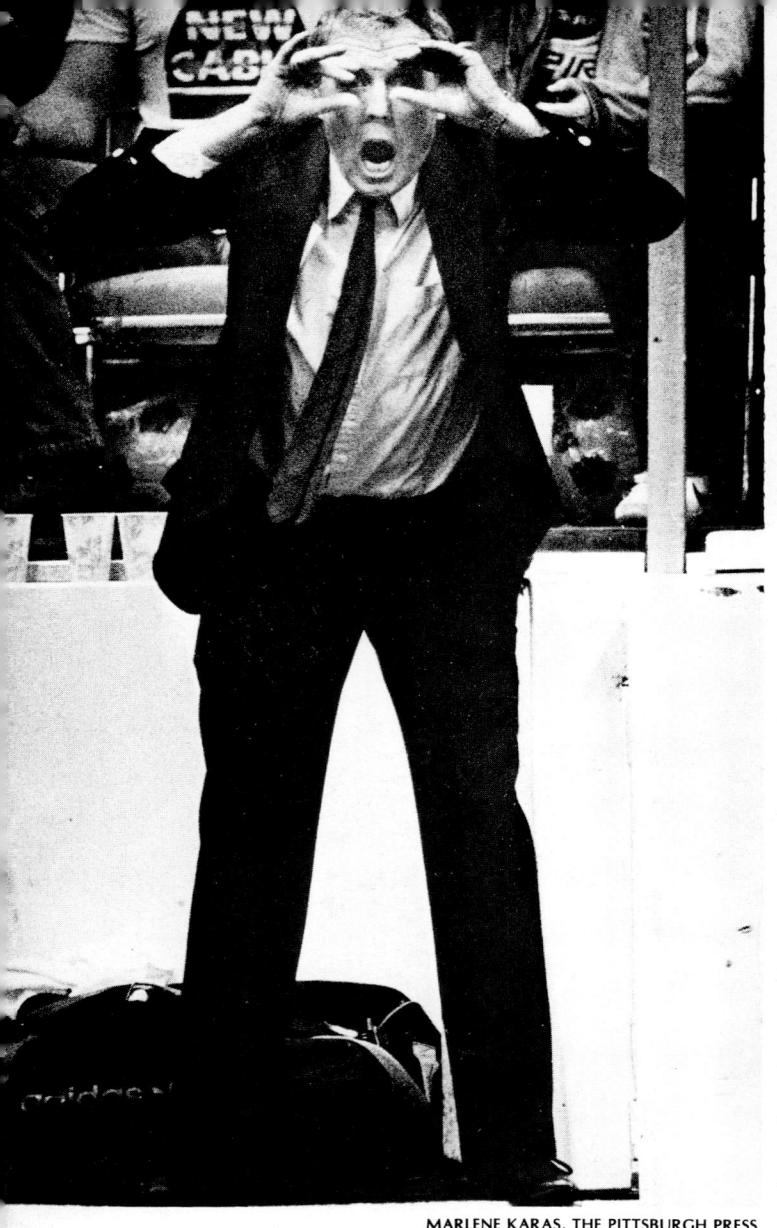

MARLENE KARAS, THE PITTSBURGH PRESS
DAVID PERRY, THE LEXINGTON (KY.) HERALD-LEADER

DAVID PETERSON, THE DES MOINES (IOWA) REGIS
RIGHT, BARRY CHIN, THE BOSTON HERA

Upper left, no words are needed as Ron Newman, coach of the San Diego Sockers, suggests officials may need glasses.

Upper right, Gary Garner, coach of Drake's basketball team in Des Moines, uses the game ball to show his unhappiness. Result: Garner drew a technical foul.

Left, Bill Baldridge, Morehead, Ky., State football coach, gets player restraint as he lets officials know what he thinks about a call.

Right, Portland Trailblazer Coach Jack Ramsey takes personal charge of Celtic Guard Dennis Johnson. The guard had stepped out of bounds. Refs got the message.

Better than soaps

Some of the greatest acting of 1985 took place on the sidelines of the nation's athletic arenas.

The actors double as coaches. Some of them are such hams that spectators often spend more time watching the sidelines than the team play.

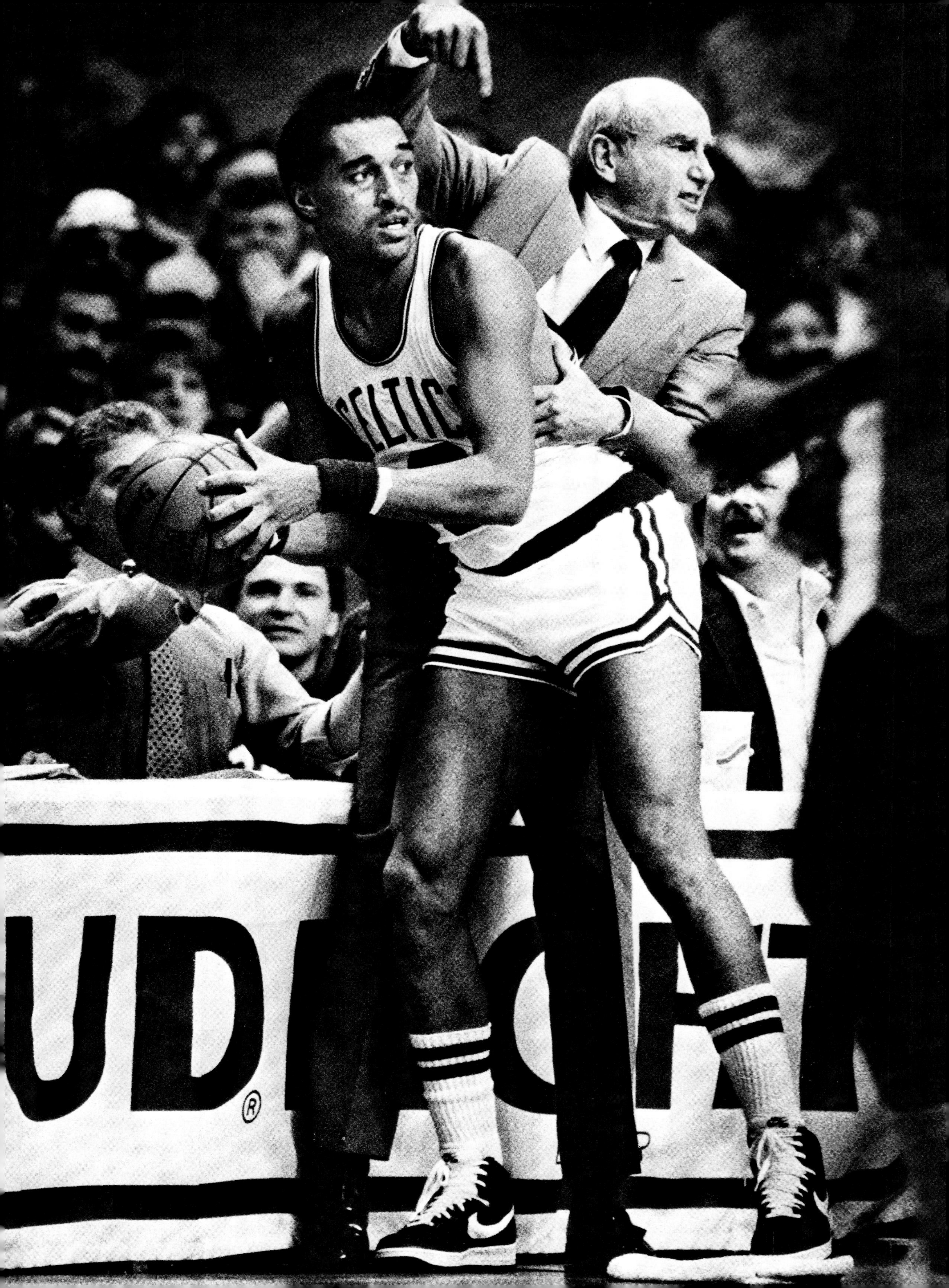

BLAIR KOOISTRA, OGDEN (UTAH) STANDARD-EXAMIN[ER]
ALEXANDER GALLARDO, THE DAILY REPORT (ONTARIO, CAL[IF.])

Above, Greg Hess, assistant football coach at Bear River, Utah, High School, emotes in response to a delay-of-game call against his team. It came during state championship playoff, which Bear River lost.

Left, Los Angeles Rams Coach John Robinson looks to the heavens for help in a game against the Green Bay Packers. Robinson's act may have helped: the Rams won.

Hamming it up

FIRST PLACE NEWSPAPER SPORTS FEATURE, SKIP PETERSON, DAYTON (OHIO) NEWSPAPERS, INC.

It was no act when Coach Rollie Massimino came off the bench in Lexington, Ky., in April 1985: His Villanova Wildcats had just upset Georgetown to win the NCAA basketball championship.

POY Quintet

Some 20,000 photographs were entered in the 43rd Pictures of the Year competition by 1,701 photographers. Winners were selected by these five judges.

ALL PHOTOS, MIKE DAVIS

MARY CARROLL MARDEN is associate picture editor of People Magazine.

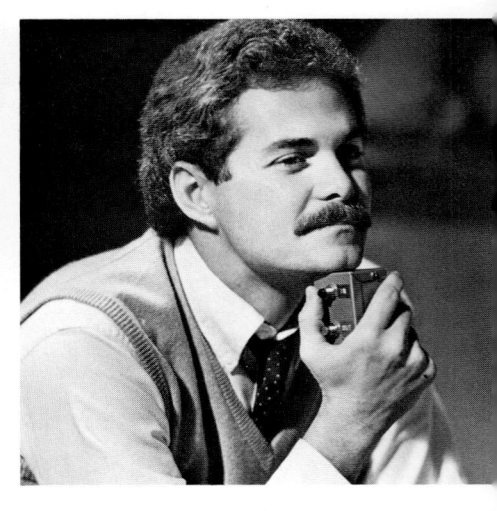

LARRY C. PRICE is a photographer with The Philadelphia Inquirer.

The 43rd —
One judge's perspective

**By Mary Carroll Marden
Associate Picture Editor
People Magazine**

For those who haven't experienced firsthand the Pictures of the Year judging held at the School of Journalism at the University of Missouri, let me set the scene.

First, the judges meet and sort of eye each other. One of the most interesting aspects of the 1986 judging, for me, was the mix of the judges:

+ Bruno Barbey, a photographer for Magnum Photos;

+ Peter Howe, photo editor of The New York Times Magazine;

+ Karen Mullarkey, photo editor of Newsweek;

+ Larry Price, Pulitzer Prize winning photographer for The Philadelphia Inquirer;

+ And me.

After the initial sizing up, judges are taken to the campus and escorted into Gannett Hall, where the judging takes place.

A lecture room, transformed into a state-of-the-art viewing room, is filled with the hush of a cathedral and with the anticipation of the students who are participating. It was just what I expected, and a little more.

Judges are led to five comfortable chairs lined up to face a counter draped in black. Each is given a buzzer with an "In" and "Out" button. (Yes, the fate of a photograph is often as fleeting as one quick push of a button.)

Votes are tabulated on a machine, and a student helper says whether a photo is in or out.

First up, the newspaper division. The orchestration of the presentation is like watching the Rockettes at Radio City Music Hall do their famous kicks. Only in this case, it's students showing photographs, smoothly, deftly, all timed to the judges' wants.

We haven't been judging long before I notice certain characteristics of the entries. First, there are too many bad photographs — really bad photographs — and this is most disturbing. We judges spent a great deal of time lamenting these entries.

True, the contest should be open to all photojournalists, but I found myself wishing that entrants would sit down and think hard about their entries:

Is it a *good* picture? Does it tell a story? Does it jump off the page (my personal criterion of worth)? Is it original? (I saw one picture that appeared to be a direct copy of a photo that had originated at and appeared in People. Coincidence? I rather doubt it.

POY is the biggest photo contest of the year, and the entries should be good photographs. I would hope that more of the photojournalists who enter would know more about picture editing, and would use that skill to determine whether a photograph should be entered. People who enter bad pictures should look at the photographs in this book and judge from them — and then keep shooting to that level, or at a higher level. Your photograph doesn't have to be

PETER HOWE is the photo editor of the New York Times Magazine

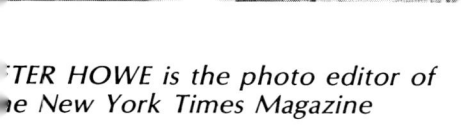

KAREN MULLARKEY joined the Newsweek staff as photo editor in 1985.

BRUNO BARBEY, a Magnum photographer, has been shooting since 1960.

beat (those are few), but it does have to be good.

Judges were struck by the unbelievable amount of repetition in the entries. I can't tell you how many shots of pile-ups of football players were viewed and groaned out of contention.

This year also saw an unusual number of entries dealing with Amish farmers, handicapped children, and pets. Again, these are fine — if they're different. Unfortunately, a large number of them were the same shot by many different photographers.

Another factor that struck all the judges: The physical quality of an entry can't help but make a difference. A bad print will rarely beat a good one. Poor quality dupes in color entries rarely measure up to top quality. A tray with upside-down or reversed transparencies is just sloppy, and after it's corrected, it's still not going to be welcomed with open arms.

Again, it's a big, important contest. Take time in printing, copying, duping, and submitting your work. Quality tells.

Not every judge perceived the photographs and the picture stories the way I did. The POY judging allowed us to edit aloud and hear our colleagues discuss their views about the entries. This was really exciting for me.

In the day-to-day reality of my life as a picture editor at People, most decisions are made quickly; stopping to think long and hard about a picture doesn't happen often.

Perhaps that's why I'm always looking for the picture that pops out at me. I have little time to think about my decisions, to figure out why one frame is better than the next. It's just automatic.

But to have a chance to hear other people verbalize opinions, and to join in the conversation, was wonderful for me.

We certainly didn't all share the same criteria for pictures. At one time I asked another judge why he hadn't liked a particular portrait, and it was because of the way the horizon had been lined up in the background. The horizon hadn't mattered to me at all — but how interesting that it did for someone else.

When I think about those six days and tens of thousands of pictures, the brief moments of boredom, the eye strain and the lower back pain are quickly forgotten. Mainly I remember the excitement of being part of the photographic community, having an opportunity to spend time with others in my field (all, incidentally, really good people), and, of course, seeing some really great work and *finally* finding out who shot some of my favorite photographs.

I discovered many new wonderful photographers all over the United States. I saw photographs at Missouri that are still with me: Tommy Hearns' eyes; Max's wife; the oldest journalist in the country; even the duck that failed its takeoff.

I also got to go back to my favorite campus hangout — Booches — where I introduced the other four judges to the best cheeseburgers in town.

Despite my problem with many of the photographs submitted, I've got to admit that 1,701 entrants do indicate that there are a lot of photographers (granted, both good and bad) who share my passion for photojournalism.

For, 1,701 (and one) people just can't be wrong.

The winners

Newspaper Photographer of the Year

Steve Ringman, San Francisco Chronicle
Second place: John Kaplan, The Pittsburgh Press
Third place: Eric Luse, San Francisco Chronicle

Magazine Photographer of the Year

Harry Benson, Life
   and
James Stanfield, National Geographic

Canon Photo Essayist Award

David C. Turnley, Detroit Free Press
Special Recognition: April Saul, The
   Philadelphia Inquirer
Special Recognition: Stephen Shames, Alicia
   Patterson Foundation

Newspaper division

SPOT NEWS
First — Lois Bernstein, The Virginian-Pilot/Ledger-Star (Norfolk), "Roadside prayer for a friend"
Second — David Parker, Yuba-Sutter Appeal-Democrat, Marysville, Calif., "Hostage rescue"
Third — Pierre Gleizes, Associated Press, "Shooting"
Honorable mention — Carol Guzy, The Miami Herald, "Omayra: a slow death"
Honorable mention — John Kaplan, The Pittsburgh Press, "A policeman's torment"

GENERAL NEWS
First — Dennis Cook, Associated Press, untitled
Second — Dennis Cook, Associated Press, untitled
Third — Gary D. Stewart, Associated Press, "Death plunge"
Honorable mention — Eric Luse, San Francisco Chronicle, "MIAs come home"

FEATURE PICTURE
First — Bob Gwaltney, The Evansville (Ind.) Press, "Go ahead and make my day"
Second — Rich Hein, The Chicago Sun-Times, "Pre-school girls"
Third — bill alkofer, Orange County Register (Santa Ana, Calif.), "Wrong way sheep"
Honorable mention — Manny Crisostomo, Detroit Free Press, "Waiting"

SPORTS ACTION
First — John Blanding, The Boston Globe, untitled
Second — Bill Wax, The Gainesville (Fla.) Sun, "Backhand smash"
Third — Christ Stewart, freelance for The Kansas City (Mo.) Times, "Going down"
Honorable mention — Charlaine Brown, Orange County Register (Santa Ana, Calif.) "Hold that bail"

SPORTS FEATURE
First — Skip Peterson, Dayton (Ohio) Newspapers, Inc., "I win"
Second — Rick Mansfield, Nashville (Tenn.) Banner, "Cop gets involved"
Third — Bruce Bisping, Minneapolis Star and Tribune, "All-Star catch"
Honorable mention — Jebb Harris, Orange County Register (Santa Ana, Calif.), "Goose hunter: the ambush"

PORTRAIT/PERSONALITY
First — Chris Hardy, San Francisco Examiner, "Grace Jones"
Second — Tom Jagoe, Los Angeles Daily News, "David Lee Roth auditions"
Third — Lance Wynn, The Grand Rapids (Mich.) Press. "Boxer Thomas Hearns"
Honorable mention — Bill Luster, The Courier-Journal

and Louisville (Ky.) Times, "Nation's oldest journalist"
Honorable mention — Jimi Lott, The Seattle Times, "Urban nomad"

PICTORIAL
First — Ted Kirk, Journal-Star Newspapers (Lincoln, Neb.), "Bovine barn art"
Second — Chris Russell, The News-Herald (Willoughby, Ohio) "Drive-in"
Third — Brant Ward, San Francisco Chronicle, "Flushing a quail"

HUMOR
First — Eric Luse, San Francisco Chronicle, "Man's best friend"
Second — George Wilhelm, Simi Valley (Calif.) Enterprise, "Unflappable"
Third — Arthur Pollock, The Boston Herald, "Too pooped to pirouette"
Honorable mention — Valerie Hodgson, freelance, "Nuka the walrus"
Honorable mention — Grant Haller, Seattle Post-Intelligencer, "Hey buddy, can you spare a crumb?"

FOOD ILLUSTRATION
First — Alan Berner, The Seattle Times, "Simply shrimp"
Second — Michael P. Franklin, San Diego (Calif.) Union-Tribune, "A splash of champagne"
Third — Scott Robinson, The Providence (R.I.) Journal, "Berry good"
Honorable mention — Stephen Crowley, The Washington Times, "What goes into mincemeat"

FASHION ILLUSTRATION
First — Craig Trumbo, The Florida Times-Union (Jacksonville), "Make a splash with red shoes"
Second — Murray Sill, The Miami Herald, "Sun (dress) spots"
Third — Erwin Gebhard, The Milwaukee Journal, "Stepping out"

EDITORIAL ILLUSTRATION
First — Jeff Alexander, The Albuquerque (N.M.) Journal, "It's scary, if you are an apple"

Second — Gary Fandel, The Des Moines (Iowa) Register, "The agony of back pain"
Third — Jim Mayfield, Springfield (Mo.) Newspapers, Inc., "Big and small"

NEWS PICTURE STORY
First — Jim Mahoney, The Boston Herald, "Goodbye, old friend"
Second — Carol Guzy, The Miami Herald, "Armero — buried alive"
Third — Bill Wax, The Gainesville (Fla.) Sun, "The execution"
Honorable mention — John Kaplan, The Pittsburgh Press, "The Philippines — crisis in Paradise"
Honorable mention — Dave Gatley, Los Angeles Times, "Dangerous prank"

FEATURE PICTURE STORY
First — April Saul, The Philadelphia Inquirer, "Survived by a daughter"
Second — Bill Luster, The Courier-Journal and Louisville (Ky.) Times, "Nation's oldest journalist"
Third — Tom Sweeney, Minneapolis Star and Tribune, "He gives strength in family tragedy"
Honorable mention — Fred Comegys, The News-Journal (Wilmington, Del.), "Amish tobacco farming"
Honorable mention — Steve Ringman, San Francisco Chronicle, "Marilyn the man"

SPORTS PICTURE STORY
First — Fred Comegys, The News-Journal (Wilmington, Del.) "Navy upsets Army"
Second — Bill Frakes, The Miami Herald, "Bye-bye, Ty!"
Third — Lui Kit Wong, San Jose (Calif.) Mercury News, "A glove and a prayer"

SELF-PRODUCED PUBLISHED PICTURE STORY
First — Kevin Clark, The Springfield News (Eugene, Ore.), "Sharing a life of hard work"
Honorable mention — Steve Mellon, The Herald (Jasper, Ind.) "Making of a team"
Honorable mention — Harry Fisher, The Morning Call (Allentown, Pa.), "Karate kids"

Magazine division

NEWS/DOCUMENTARY
First — Gamma-Liaison for Time, "Hijackers of TWA 847"
Second — Frank Fournier, Contact Press Images, "The agony of Omayra"
Third — George Widman, Time, "Vigil on rooftop"
Honorable mention — Andy Levin, freelance, "Born in ..."

FEATURE
First — Bruce Davidson, New York Magazine, "Hunting the wolf packs"
Second — Lynn Johnson, A Day in the Life of Japan, "Rusty baths"
Third — Diana Walker, Time, "Surprise!"
Honorable mention — Dean Conger, National Geographic, "Monks at breakfast"

Magazine winners (cont'd)

Honorable mention — Richard Kalvar, Magnum for Connoisseur, "Tokyo made easy"

SPORTS
First — Mickey Pfleger, freelance, "Flying Ozzie"
Second — Joe McNally, freelance, "Backyard game"
Third — Peter Menzel, freelance, "Flyaway"

PORTRAIT/PERSONALITY
First — Jon Warren, World Concern, "Hammock refugee"
Second — Harry Benson, Life, "King of Spain"
Third — Annie Leibovitz, Newsweek, "Nude Sting"

PICTORIAL
First — Cotton Coulson, National Geographic, "Kansas landscape"
Second — James Sugar, National Geographic, "Eruption, Kiluea"
Third — James Stanfield, National Geographic, "Day of Epiphany"
Honorable Mention — James Stanfield, National Geographic, "Good Friday — St. Peter's Square"

SCIENCE/NATURAL HISTORY
First — Peter Menzel, freelance, "Tehachapi windmills"
Second — Stephen Krasemann, National Geographic, "A leopard has ..."
Third — Stephen Krasemann, National Geographic, "A flock of ..."
Honorable mention — Frans Lanting, National Wildlife, "Shore leave"

ILLUSTRATION
First — Gary Chapman, The Courier-Journal and Louisville (Ky.) Times, untitled
Second — Gilles Tapie, Time, "Miyake's coat"
Third — Brian Hagiwara, Connoisseur, "Edible avant-garde"

PICTURE STORY
First — Andy Levin, freelance, "Bitter harvest"
Second — Michael Coyne, Newsweek, "Iran under the Ayatollah"
Third — Stephen Shames, Alicia Patterson Foundation, "Homeless"
Honorable mention — Jodi Cobb, National Geographic, "A day in the life of Japan: Geisha life"
Honorable mention — Wayne Source, Newsweek, "Striking back"

Editing awards

BEST USE OF PHOTOGRAPHS BY A NEWSPAPER UNDER 30,000
Claremont (Calif.) Courier

BEST USE OF PHOTOGRAPHS BY A NEWSPAPER OVER 30,000
St. Petersburg (Fla.) Times

NEWSPAPER PICTURE EDITOR AWARD
First — Dick Bell, The Philadelphia Inquirer
Special recognition — Randy Cox, The Hartford (Conn.) Courant
Special recognition — Mike Healy, San Jose (Calif.) Mercury News
Special recognition — Kristine Snipes, The Sacramento (Calif.) Bee

NEWSPAPER MAGAZINE PICTURE EDITOR AWARD
Bill Marr, "Inquirer," The Philadelphia Inquirer

BEST USE OF PHOTOGRAPHS BY A MAGAZINE
First — Life
Special recognition: National Geographic Traveler

NEWSPAPER PICTURE EDITOR AWARD
DICK BELL, THE PHILADELPHIA INQUIRER

BEST USE OF PHOTOGRAPHS BY A NEWSPAPER OVER 30,000
ST. PETERSBURG (FLA.) TIMES

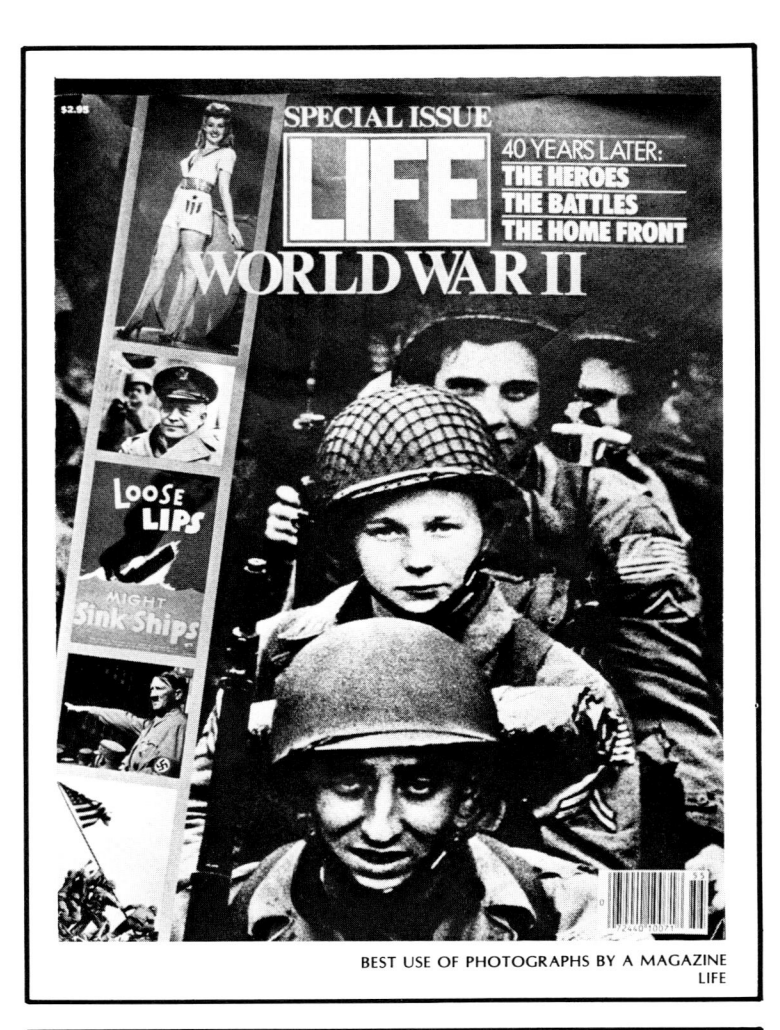

BEST USE OF PHOTOGRAPHS BY A MAGAZINE
LIFE

BEST USE OF PHOTOGRAPHS BY A NEWSPAPER UNDER 30,000
CLAREMONT (CALIF.) COURIER

NEWSPAPER MAGAZINE PICTURE EDITOR AWARD
BILL MARR, THE PHILADELPHIA INQUIRER

237

Index to photographers

ADASKAVEG, MIKE
Journal Inquirer (Manchester, Conn.)
p. 143

AHRENS, JUDY
The Suffolk Times (Greenport, N.Y.)
p. 71

ALCOCK, AMANDA
Chicago Sun-Times
p. 111

ALEXANDER, JEFF
Albuquerque (N.M.) Journal
p. 145, 172

bill alkofer
The Orange County Register, (Santa Ana, Calif.)
p. 155

ANDERSON, KATHY
The Times Picayune Publishing Corp. (New Orleans, La.)
p. 21

BADMAN, JOHN
Alton (Ill.) Telegraph
p. 98

BARGER, REBECCA
Freelance, Willow Grove, Pa.
p. 27

BARRERA, JOE M. JR.
San Antonio (Texas) Express and News
p. 158

BATSON, WILLIAM H.
Omaha (Neb.) World-Herald
p. 226

BAYTOFF, MICHAEL A.
Atlantic City (N.J.) Press
p. 138

BECKLEY, CHUCK
San Antonio (Texas) Light
p. 176

BEDELL, ROBBIE
The Miami Herald
p. 170

BENSON, HARRY
Life Magazine, New York
p. 2, 42, 43

BERMAN, CHUCK
Chicago Tribune
p. 142

BERNER, ALAN
The Seattle Times
p. 148, 179

BERNSTEIN, LOIS
The Virginian-Pilot and The Ledger-Star (Norfolk)
p. 102

BERTEAUX, BRYAN S.
The Times-Picayune Publishing Corp. (New Orleans, La.)
p. 72, 103

BISPING, BRUCE
Minneapolis Star and Tribune
p. 201

BLANDING, JOHN
The Boston Globe
p. 225

BOCKWINKEL, SHERRY
Bellevue (Wash.) Journal-American
p. 105

BORCHERS, KAREN T.
San Jose (Calif.) Mercury News
p. 75

BOSTON, BERNIE
Los Angeles Times
p. 104

BRONSTEIN, PAULA
Hartford (Conn.) Courant
p. 70, 118

BROOKS, DUDLEY M.
The Washington Post
p. 49

BYER, RENEE
The Peoria (Ill.) Journal Star
p. 65

CHAPMAN, GARY S.
Sunday Magazine of The Louisville (Ky.) Courier-Journal
p. 156

CHIN, BARRY J.
The Boston Herald
p. 229

CHINN, PAUL
Los Angeles Herald Examiner
p. 201

CHRISTOPHER, RUSSELL
The News-Herald, (Willoughby, Ohio)
p. 145

CHUCKOVICH, MILAN
The Columbian (Vancouver, Wash.)
p. 110, 176

CLERY, MARC
The Miami Herald
p. 108

COBB, JODI
National Geographic
p. 46

COMEGYS, FRED
The News-Journal Co. (Wilmington, Del.)
p. 184, 210, 211, 212, 213

CONRAD, FRED R.
The New York Times
p. 175

COOK, CHUCK
The Times-Picayune Publishing Corp.
(New Orleans, La.)
p. 72

COOK, DENNIS
Associated Press
p. 49, 88

CORTES, RON
The News-Journal Co. (Wilmington, Del.)
p. 206

COULSON, COTTON R.
National Geographic
p. 41

COURSON, J. GILLIS
Florida Today (Cocoa)
p. 56

COURTNEY, MARK
The Post-Crescent (Appleton, Wis.)
p. 1, 172

COYNE, MICHAEL
Freelance (Victoria, Australia)
p. 40

CREIGHTON, BILL
Reuters
p. 203

CRUZE, TOM
Chicago Sun-Times
p. 100, 167

DAVIDSON, BRUCE
New York Magazine
p. 160

DELANEY, MICHAEL
The Miami News
p. 52

deMolina, Raul
Freelance (Coral Gables, Fla.)
p. 68

DICKMAN, JAY
Dallas Times Herald
p. 20

DIDLICK, NICK
Reuters
p. 227

DiROCCO, HENRY J.
Los Angeles Times
p. 143

DODGE, THOMAS
Freelance (Truman, Minn.)
p. 59

duCILLE, MICHEL
The Miami Herald
p. 16

DUNCAN, MARK
Associated Press
p. 67

DUNN, JOHN
Journal Inquirer (Manchester, Conn.)
p. 171

DURELL, ROBERT E.
The Fresno (Calif.) Bee
p. 103

DZIEKAN, JOHN
Chicago Tribune
p. 99

EATON, CHARLES F. JR.
Winston-Salem (N.C.) Journal
p. 190

EGGITT, JOHN
Reuters
p. 177

ENDLICHER, DIETER
Associated Press
p. 92

EVANS, MELVIN C. JR.
Omaha (Neb.) World-Herald
p. 60

EWEN, MICHAEL
Tallahassee (Fla.) Democrat
p. 69

EYESTONE, ALLEN
The Palm Beach (Fla.) Post and Evening Times
p. 221

FANDEL, GARY P.
The Des Moines (Iowa) Register
p. 145

FERRO, RICARDO J.
St. Petersburg (Fla.) Times
p. 178

FISHER, DON
The Morning Call (Allentown, Pa.)
p. 138, 162

FITZGERALD, CHRISTOPHER
Middlesex News (Framingham, Mass.)
p. 158, 173

FITZGERALD, RALPH P.
Freelance (Norfolk, Va.)
p. 123

FITZMAURICE, DEANNE
San Francisco Examiner
p. 12

FONG, GARY E.
San Francisco Chronicle
p. 142

FORBES, JAMES
St. Louis Post-Dispatch
p. 7, 10

FORENCICH, SAM
The Peninsula Times-Tribune (Palo Alto, Calif.)
p. 98

FOX, FRED
The Tampa (Fla.) Tribune-Times
p. 69

FOURNIER, FRANK
Contact Press Images, New York
p. 14

FRAKES, BILL
The Miami Herald
p. 194, 195, 196, 197, 198, 199

FRANKLIN, MICHAEL
San Diego (Calif.) Union/Tribune
p. 148

FUCHS, AL
The Orange County Register (Santa Ana, Calif.)
p. 141

GALLACHER, MICHAEL D.
Missoulian (Missoula, Mont.)
p. 141

GALLARDO, ALEXANDER
The Daily Report (Ontario, Calif.)
p. 230

GANTER, J. CARL
The Courier-Journal and Louisville (Ky.) Times
p. 174

GAPS, JOHN III
Associated Press
p. 119

GEBHARD, ERWIN
The Milwaukee Journal
p. 149

GEHMAN, RAYMOND
The Virginian-Pilot and The Ledger-Star (Norfolk)
p. 144

GEHRZ, JIM
Daily Globe (Worthington, Minn.)
p. 172

GEIL, KEVIN
Round Rock (Texas) Leader
p. 147

GLEIZES, PIERRE
Associated Press
p. 79

GOEBEL, ROB
Indianapolis (Ind.) Star
p. 176

GOLD, ARNOLD
The Times Leader (Wilkes-Barre, Pa.)
p. 139

GOLDSMITH, SCOTT
The Courier-Journal and Louisville (Ky.) Times
p. 166

GONZALEZ, EDUARDO
Associated Press
p. 16

GOULD, DANIEL
Worcester (Mass.) Telegram and Gazette
p. 83

GOULDING, MICHAEL
Los Angeles Daily News
p. 107

GREENE, JEFF
The Journal (Lorain, Ohio)
p. 140, 170

GRIESEDIECK, JUDY
San Jose (Calif.) Mercury News
p. 139

GROSSMAN, G. LOIE
Philadelphia Daily News
p. 174

GUZY, CAROL
The Miami Herald
p. 17

GWALTNEY, BOB
The Evansville (Ind.) Press
p. 136

HAGIWARA, BRIAN
Connoisseur Magazine
p. 157

HALL, DURELL
The Courier-Journal and Louisville (Ky.) Times
p. 175

HALLER, GRANT M.
Seattle Post-Intelligencer
p. 117, 146

HANDSCHUH, DAVID
New York Post
p. 78

HARBUS, RICHARD L.
United Press International
p. 91

HARDY, CHRIS
San Francisco Examiner
p. 166

HARPER, ACEY C.
U.S.A. Today
p. 165

HAWLEY, THOMAS J.
The Monroe (Mich.) Evening News
p. 65

HEIN, RICH
Chicago Sun-Times
p. 137

HERTZBERG, MARK
The Journal Times (Racine, Wis.)
p. 55

HILLE, ED
The Philadelphia Inquirer
p. 21

HODGSON, VALERIE
Freelance (Brooklyn, N.Y.)
p. 151

INOUE, ITSUO
Associated Press
p. 54

ISAACS, CHARLES
The Philadelphia Inquirer
p. 25

ISMAIL, NABIL
Agence France-Presse
p. 49

JACKSON, TED
The Times-Picayune Publishing Corp.
(New Orleans, La.)
p. 12, 192

JAGOE, TOM
Los Angeles Daily News
p. 164

JOHNSON, BRUCE
The Philadelphia Daily News
pg. 24

JOHNSON, LYNN
A Day in the Life (New York)
p. 160

JONES, STEVE
Ogden (Utah) Standard-Examiner
p. 140

JORDAN, ROBERT
University of Mississippi
p. 187

KAPLAN, JOHN
The Pittsburgh Press
p. 47, 74, 75, 76, 77, 80, 221

KARAS, MARLENE
The Pittsburgh Press
p. 228

KASAHARA, KATSUMI
Associated Press
p. 54

KELSEY, THOMAS
Los Angeles Times
p. 4

KELSH, NICK
The Philadelphia Inquirer
p. 98

KIRK, TED
Journal Star Printing Co (Lincoln, Neb.)
p. 47

KIRN, JONATHAN
The Daily Herald (Arlington Heights, Ill.)
p. 200

KITAGAKI, PAUL, JR.
San Francisco Examiner
p. 8, 12, 13

KLEPITSCH, JIM
Chicago Sun-Times
p. 93

KNOTT, JANET
The Boston Globe
p. 29

KODEY, WAYNE C.
Las Vegas (Nev.) Review-Journal
p. 215

KOENIG, GLENN
Freelance (Fullerton, Calif.)
p. 82

KOOISTRA, BLAIR
Ogden (Utah) Standard-Examiner
p. 230

KRAL, JON
The Miami Herald
p. 158

KRASEMANN, STEPHEN J.
Freelance (Sedona, Ariz.)
p. 153

LAMAA
Agence France-Presse
p. 121

LANDERS, THOMAS E.
The Boston Globe
p. 16

LARAGY, JIM
Gannett Rochester (N.Y.)

238

ewspapers
186

ARSON, FREDERIC
n Francisco Chronicle
31

AURIE, JIM
s Vegas (Nev.) Review-Journal
214

AW, DENIS W.
aherty Newspapers (Seattle, ash.)
187, back cover

E, CRAIG
n Francisco Examiner
30

E, RICHARD
ew York Newsday
125

EN, SARAH
e Philadelphia Inquirer
126, 127, 128, 129

PSKI, RICHARD
ashington Post
124

NG, JOHN C. JR.
artford (Conn.) Courant
71

NGSTREATH, DAVID
ssociated Press
79

SE, ERIC
n Francisco Chronicle
9, 12, 13, 91, 101, 154, 167,
8

STER, BILL
e Courier-Journal and
uisville (Ky.) Times
51, 132, 133, 134, 135

ONS, WILLIAM
ew Castle (Pa.) News
67

ADISON, CASEY
e Columbian (Vancouver, ash.)
87

AHONEY, BOB
racuse (N.Y.) Newspapers
29

AHONEY, JIM
e Boston Herald
84, 85

ANSFIELD, RICK
ashville (Tenn.) Banner
193

ATHER, JAY B.
e Courier-Journal and
uisville (Ky.) Times
116

AYFIELD, JIM
ringfield (Mo.) Newspapers
144

cCOY, JAMES P.
agara Gazette (Niagara Falls, Y.)
193

cDONALD, DENNIS A.
rlington County Times
illingboro, N.J.)
4

cDONALD, MICHELE
e Virginian-Pilot and The
dger-Star (Norfolk)
162

cDONOGH, PAT
e Courier-Journal and
uisville (Ky.) Times
100

cKAY, RICK
x Newspapers (Washington, C.)
90

cLENDON, LENNOX
ssociated Press
11

cNALLY, JOE
eelance (New York)
152

ELENA, JOE
e Peninsula Times-Tribune
alo Alto, Calif.)
150

ELLON, STEVE
e Herald (Jasper, Ind.)
116

ENDENHALL, JIM
e Orange County Register

(Santa Ana, Calif.)
p. 206

MENZEL, PETER J.
Freelance (Napa, Calif.)
p. 152, 153

MERIPOL, ART
Arkansas Gazette (Little Rock)
p. 63

MERLIAC, HERVE
Associated Press
p. 55, 120

MONTESINOS, IVAN
Agence France-Presse
p. 90

MORRIS, LARRY
Washington Post
p. 88

MOSCONI, BRUNO
Associated Press
p. 104

MYERS, KEITH A.
The Kansas City (Mo.) Times
pg. 202

MYERS, ORVILLE JR.
Monterey (Calif.) Peninsula Herald
p. 28

MYRENT, DEBRA
Freelance (Culver City, Calif.)
p. 102

NANDELL, ROBERT A.
The Des Moines (Iowa) Register
p. 155

NESIUS, STEVEN J.
Gainesville (Fla.) Sun
p. 208

NICKERSON, STEVE
The Lexington (Ky.) Herald-Leader
p. 141

NIEMEIR, FRANK
The Kansas City (Mo.) Times
p. 58, 61, 62, 189

NUSS, CHERYL
San Jose (Calif.) Mercury News
p. 31

O'HARA, PAM SMITH
The Miami Herald
p. 204

O'NEILL, PAUL
The Mesa (Ariz.) Tribune
p. 151

PAQUIN, DENNIS
Reuters
p. 89

PARKER, DAVID
Yuba-Sutter Appeal-Democrat
(Marysville, Calif.)
p. 81, front cover

PAVUCHAK, ROBERT J.
The Pittsburgh Press
p. 64

PEARMAN, REGINALD
The Tribune (Oakland, Calif.)
p. 110

PENCH, RANDY
The Sacrament (Calif.) Bee
p. 186

PERRY, DAVID
The Lexington (Ky.) Herald-Leader
p. 228

PETERS, GREG
The Hutchinson (Kan.) News
p. 192

PETERSON, DAVID
The Des Moines (Iowa) Register
p. 228

PETERSON, SKIP
Dayton (Ohio) Newspapers
p. 231

PFLEGER, MICKEY
Freelance (San Francisco)
p. 152

PINNEO, JOANNA B.
Associated Press
p. 19

PODGORSKI, AL
Chicago Sun-Times
p. 162

POLLOCK, ARTHUR
The Boston Herald
p. 137

POLO, WILLIAM

The Boston Herald
p. 173

PORTER, COLE
Seattle Times
p. 177

POWERS, CAROL T.
Washington Times
p. 31

PRICE, LARRY
The Philadelphia Inquirer
p. 66

PRICE, TOMMY
The Virginian-Pilot and The Ledger-Star (Norfolk)
p. 122

RAPPING, ANACLETO
Los Angeles Times
p. 165

REDDY, PATRICK
The Cincinnati Post
p. 66

REYNOLDS, GEORGE
Philadelphia Daily News
p. 222

REYNOLDS, GUY A.
Morning Advocate (Baton Rouge, La.)
p. 225

RICKMAN, RICK
The Orange County Register
(Santa Ana, Calif.)
p. 123

RIEDEL, CHARLIE A.
The Hays (Kan.) Daily News
p. 58

RINGHAM, BOB
Chicago Sun-Times
p. 93

RINGMAN, STEVE
San Francisco Chronicle
p. 82, 164, 167, 168, 169, 180,
181, 182, 183, 204, 205

RIVENBARK, MAURICE
St. Petersburg (Fla.) Times
p. 73

ROBINSON, SCOTT G.
The Providence (R.I.) Journal
p. 148

RONDOU, MICHAEL
Long Beach (Calif.) Press-Telegram
p. 111

ROOT, DAN
Missoulian (Missoula, Mont.)
p. 221

RUEBSAMEN, JAMES
Los Angeles Herald Examiner
p. 207, 215

RUSSELL, CHRIS
The News-Herald (Willoughby, Ohio)
p. 145

RYAN, DAVID
The Boston Globe
p. 174

SAIIDI, JAMAL
Associated Press
p. 48, 121

SALYER, TOM
United Press International
p. 18

SANCETTA, AMY
Associated Press
p. 26, 223

SARICOSTAS, ARISTOTLE
Associated Press
p. 120

SAUL, APRIL
The Philadelphia Inquirer
p. 94, 95, 96, 97

SCHECHTER, ELIOT JAY
Ft. Lauderdale (Fla.) News
p. 73

SCHMIDT, RICHARD
The Sacramento (Calif.) Bee
p. 18

SCHREIBER, DAVID
The Sun (San Bernardino, Calif.)
p. 30

SEIB, AL
Los Angeles Times
p. 136

SEIFERT, DAN
The Kansas City (Mo.) Star
p. 142

SHAMES, STEPHEN
Alicia Patterson Foundation (New York)
p. 161

SHAW, JEFF
Dallas Times Herald
p. 151

SHECKLER, JOHN F.
Standard Times (New Bedford, Mass.)
p. 71

SILL, MURRAY
The Miami Herald
p. 149

SINES, SCOTT R.
San Antonio (Texas) Express-News
p. 9

SLUDER, MARK B.
The Charlotte (N.C.) Observer
p. 166, 220

SMITH, KURT E.
Seattle Post-Intelligencer
p. 86

SOLTES, HARLEY
The Seattle Times
p. 86, 87, 117

SONGER, JOE
Nashville (Tenn.) Banner
p. 50

SOURCE, WAYNE
Newsweek Magazine
p. 46

SPENCER, DAVID
The Sun-Tattler (Hollywood, Fla.)
p. 170

STANFIELD, JAMES
National Geographic
p. 44, 45

STARNES, JOHN A.
The Pittsburgh Press
p. 173

STEAGALL, LARRY
The Bremerton (Wash.) Sun
p. 99

STEINBRUNNER, CHARLES
The Journal Herald (Dayton, Ohio)
p. 51

STEINKAMP, SUSAN V.
Syracuse (N.Y.) Newspapers
p. 150

STEINMETZ, WILLIAM E.
The Philadelphia Inquirer
p. 22

STEWART, CHRIS
Freelance (Manhattan, Kan.)
p. 220

STEWART, CHRISTOPHER
San Francisco Chronicle
p. 209

STEWART, GARY D.
Associated Press
p. 105

STONE, NANCY
The Daily Herald (Arlington Heights, Ill.)
p. 62

STRACHAN, ERIC
Naples (Fla.) Daily News
p. 101

STRICKSTEIN, IRA
The Houston Post
p. 15

STUBBLEBINE, RAY
Associated Press
p. 163

SUAU, ANTHONY
Black Star
p. 14

SUGAR, JAMES
National Geographic
p. 41, 161

SWEENEY, TOM
Minneapolis Star and Tribune
p. 130, 131

TAPIE, GILLIS
Time Magazine
p. 157

THUMMA, BARRY
Associated Press
p. 122

TIERNAN, BILL
The Virginian-Pilot and The Ledger-Star (Norfolk)
p. 220

TILLERY, DAVID C.
San Angelo (Texas) Standard Times
p. 147

TOMBAUGH, BRIAN S.
The Journal (Lorain, Ohio)
p. 191

TRUMBO, CRAIG
The Florida Times-Union
(Jacksonville)
p. 149

TURNLEY, DAVID
Detroit Free Press
p. 33, 34, 35, 36, 37, 38, 39

VALERIO, VICKI
The Philadelphia Inquirer
p 23, 26

VALLBONA, NURI
Fort Worth (Texas) Star-Telegram
p. 15

VALLONE, CHARLES S.
The Journal Times (Racine, Wis.)
p. 171

VAN DYKE, TOM
San Jose (Calif.) Mercury News
p. 106

VERGARI, MARK
Westchester Rockland Newspapers
(White Plains, N.Y.)
p. 223

WADE, BILL
The Pittsburgh Press
p. 64

WALKER, DIANA
Time Magazine
p. 160

WARD, BRANT
San Francisco Chronicle
p. 154

WARREN, JON
World Concern Magazine
(Seattle)
p. 161

WAX, BILL
Gainesville (Fla.) Sun
p. 68, 112, 113, 114, 115, 224

WEBER, GARY
Agence France-Presse
p. 92

WEISENBURGER, SKIP
The Middletown (Conn.) Press
p. 106

WELLER, BONNIE
Delaware State News (Dover)
p. 70

WELLS, DOUG
The Des Moines (Iowa) Register
pg. 205

WIDMAN, GEORGE
Associated Press
p. 23, 25

WILHELM, GEORGE
Simi Valley (Calif.) Enterprise
p. 178

WILLIAMS, GERALD
The Philadelphia Inquirer
p. 22

WILLIAMSON, MICHAEL
The Sacramento (Calif.) Bee
p. 8

WILSON, JIM
The New York Times
p. 18, 19

WIRTZ, MICHAEL
Dallas Times Herald
p. 56

WONG, LIU KIT
San Jose (Calif.) Mercury News
p. 216, 217, 218, 219

WOO, DAVID
Dallas Morning News
p. 6

WYNN, LANCE
The Grand Rapids (Mich.) Press
p. 172, 214

YONAN, DENNIS K.
Hartford (Conn.) Courant
p. 70

ZALAZNIK, DAVID
The Cedar Rapids (Iowa) Gazette
p. 59

ZENT, SHERMAN D.
The Palm Beach (Fla.) Post
p. 89, 109

239

The Best of
PHOTOJOURNALISM

Presented annually by the National Press Photographers Association and the University of Missouri School of Journalism

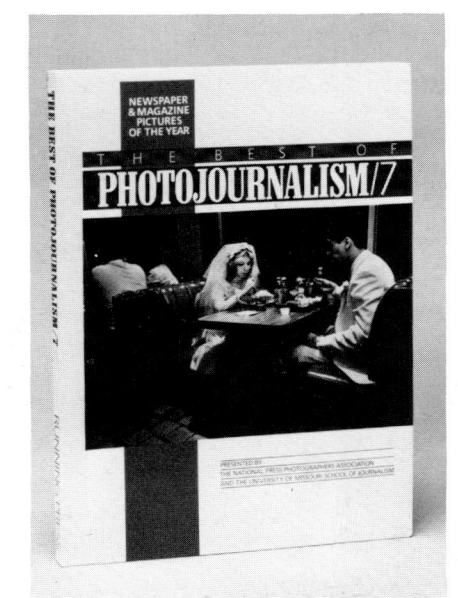

The Best of Photojournalism/7
$12.95

The Best of Photojournalism/9
$14.95

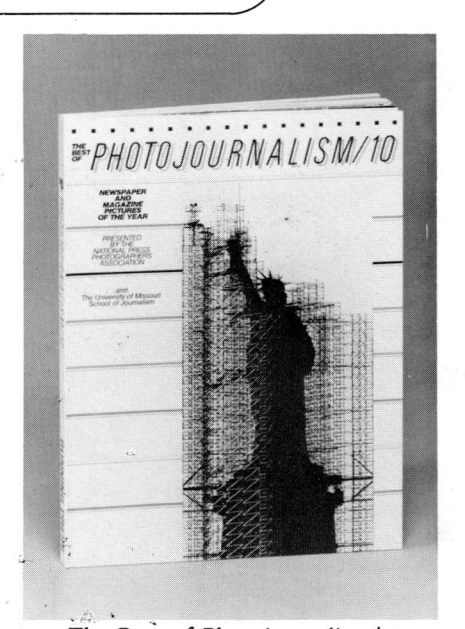

The Best of Photojournalism/10
$14.95

A very limited number of the previous editions of "the best annual publication of photojournalistic work"* are still available— but are expected to go out of print shortly.

Each volume measures 9 inches by 12 inches, and is 256 pages, paperbound.

If your local booksellers do not have copies of these past editions in stock, they can order them for you. Or you can order them by mail direct from the publisher. Send the proper amount for each book desired, plus $1.50 per volume for postage and handling, to:

RUNNING PRESS
Book Publishers
125 South 22nd Street
Philadelphia, Pennsylvania 19103

*The Bellingham Herald